Studies in Writing & Rhetoric

IN 1980, THE CONFERENCE ON COLLEGE COMPOSITION AND COMmunication perceived a need for providing publishing opportunities for monographs that were too long for publication in its journal and too short for the typical scholarly books published by the National Council of Teachers of English. The Studies in Writing and Rhetoric series was conceived, and a Publications Committee established.

Monographs to be considered for publication may be speculative, theoretical, historical, analytical, or empirical studies; research reports; or other works contributing to a better understanding of composition and communication, including interdisciplinary studies or studies in related disciplines. The SWR series will exclude textbooks, unrevised dissertations, book-length manuscripts, course syllabi, lesson plans, and collections of previously published material.

Any teacher-writer interested in submitting a work for publication in this series should submit either a prospectus and sample manuscript or a full manuscript to the NCTE Director of Publications, 1111 Kenyon Road, Urbana, IL 61801. Accompanied by sample manuscript, a prospectus should contain a rationale, a definition of readership within the CCCC constituency, comparison with related extant publications, a tentative table of contents, an estimate of length in double-spaced 8½ × 11 sheets, and the date by which full manuscript can be expected. Manuscripts should range from 100 to 170 typed manuscript pages.

The present work serves as a model for further SWR monographs.

           Paul O'Dea
           NCTE Director of Publications

Computers & Composing: How the New Technologies Are Changing Writing

*Jeanne W. Halpern
& Sarah Liggett*

WITH A FOREWORD BY EDWARD P. J. CORBETT

Published for the Conference on College
Composition and Communication

SOUTHERN ILLINOIS UNIVERSITY PRESS
Carbondale and Edwardsville

Stafford Library
Columbia College
10th and Rodgers
Columbia, MO 65216

Research described in this book was supported by grants from the Purdue Research Foundation and the School of Humanities, Social Science, and Education at Purdue University.

Production of works in this series has been partly funded by the Conference on College Composition and Communication of the National Council of Teachers of English.

Copyright © 1984 by the Conference on College Composition and Communication

All rights reserved

Printed in the United States of America
Designed by Design for Publishing, Bob Nance
Production supervised by Kathleen Giencke

Library of Congress Cataloging in Publication Data

Halpern, Jeanne W.
  Computers & composing.

  (Studies in writing and rhetoric)
  Bibliography: p.
  1. English language—Rhetoric—Study and teaching.
2. English language—Rhetoric—Data processing.
3. Authorship—Data processing. 4. Word processing.
I. Liggett, Sarah. II. Title. III. Title: Computers and composing. IV. Series.
PE1404.H34 1984   808'.042'07   83-9300
ISBN 0-8093-1146-1

87 86 85 84 4 3 2 1

To Our Sine Qua Non on This Project
Ann Marie Hedgecough

Contents

FOREWORD by Edward P. J. Corbett   xi

PREFACE   xv

1. The New Technologies Are Changing Written Communication   1
    Responding to Technological Change   2
    Defining the Scope of the Problem   4
    Investigating the New Communication Systems   4
    Narrowing the Research Focus   8

2. The New Systems Require New Composing Strategies   13
    Purpose: Investigating Critical Features   14
    Methods: Analyzing Processes and Products   15
    Results: Composing on Dictation Systems   19
    Discussion: Identifying Critical Features   22
        Addressing Dual Audiences   23
        Using Task-Responsive Planning Strategies   25
        Making Ad Hoc Plans   30
        Incorporating Oral Delivery Skills   34
        Using Auditory as Well as Visual Review Procedures   36
        Collaborating with People and Equipment Throughout the Composing Process   39
    Conclusions: Implications for Teaching and Research   41
        Questions about Teaching   42
        Questions for Research   45
    Responding to Change   45

viii Contents

3. Teachers Can Use Research about the New Systems in Freshman and Advanced Composition Classes 47
   Defining Teaching Goals to Introduce the New Systems in Freshman Composition Classes 48
   Task Environment 49
   Planning 51
   Translating Plans into Writing 52
   Reviewing 54
   Designing and Using a Specific Performance Objective 58
   Evaluating the Unit Impressionistically 61
   Defining Teaching Goals to Introduce the New Systems in Advanced Composition Classes 62
   Task Environment 63
   Planning 64
   Translating 67
   Reviewing 69
   Using a Specific Performance Objective and Assignment 71
   Conducting Research on the Effectiveness of Pedagogy 72
   Design, Subjects, and Treatments 73
   Evaluation Methods and Results 75
   Discussion 77

4. The New Technologies Offer Challenging Prospects for Research 79
   Suggesting New Directions for Productive Research 80
   Developing Interdisciplinary Projects 81
   Choosing Research Methods 82
   Selecting Research Settings, Clientele, and Topics 84
   Establishing Useful Connections Between the Classroom and the World at Large 86
   Justifying Professional Pursuits 88

   APPENDIXES 93
A. Interview List: Administrators, Systems Supervisors, and Transcriptionists 93
B. Questions on Structured Interview Form 96
C. The Process of Dictation 97
D. Segment of Edited First Draft, Summary of Actions 99
E. Segment of Final Copy, Summary of Actions 101
F. Sample of First-time-final Letter 103
G. Flower and Hayes' Model of Composing in Writing 105
H. Using Audio Mail: An Assignment 106
I. Audio Mail: A User's Guide 108
J. Students' Responses to Unit on Audio Mail 109

K. Sources for Teaching Dictation   110
L. McCoy's Memo, Used in Dictation Assignment   112
M. Guide to Planning Effective Dictation   113
N. Personnel Director's Memo, Used in Dictation Experiment   115

NOTES   117

SELECTED BIBLIOGRAPHY   137

Tables

1. Test for Differences Between Groups, Holistic Scores   76
2. Test for Differences Between Groups, Analytic Features   76

Foreword
Edward P. J. Corbett

AS HAPPENS IN ANY PERIOD OF TRANSITION, SOME PEOPLE WILL have to be dragged kicking and screaming into the twenty-first century. Some of those kickers and screamers will undoubtedly be teachers of English who have been unwilling or unable to adjust to the changes and challenges resulting from the new electronic means of communication. If they continue to be recalcitrant, they will very quickly become museum pieces, as quaint and as outmoded as the quill pen. Meanwhile, computers and word processors will become as much a part of the furnishings of the classroom as chalkboards are now, and "computer literacy" will become the new buzz term in the schools.

In this monograph, Jeanne W. Halpern and Sarah Liggett, two farseeing English teachers, are serving as heralds of the new age. They want to acquaint us with the potentialities of the electronic hardware, to show us what changes writers may have to make in their composing habits, and to inform us of the changes we may have to make in our syllabi in order to prepare our students for the demands of the electronic world. As they say in their opening chapter, "we will have to determine the kinds of research and classroom practice that will integrate the new technology into our theory and our pedagogy, while maintaining the humanistic values of our discipline."

In the first chapter, Halpern and Liggett talk about the capabilities, and the rapidly growing use in the business and professional world, of such electronic gadgetry as telecommunication systems, which make possible give-and-take lectures and conferences involving hundreds of people assembled in widely scattered cities and connected by means of video and audio hookups; audio mail systems, which allow callers to leave a voice message when the person being called is not in; and electronic mail systems, which can transmit a written message from an office in New York City to an office in Dubuque, Iowa, in a matter of seconds. But the technology that Halpern and Liggett are most interested in is the development of new dictation machines and word processors powered by microcomputers.

In the second chapter, the authors describe what they learned about the dictation/word processing systems from an extensive review of the literature and from 28 structured interviews with users and trainers of users in various business sites across the nation. From what they learned in their descriptive research project, they outline for us in their third chapter the curricula we will have to devise for our composition classrooms if we want to enable our students to be not just efficient operators of the machines but effective composers of prose on those machines. In their final chapter, they tell us about an exciting day-long international teleconference they participated in, an electronic symposium involving over 1,200 on-the-job writers who listened to lectures and engaged in transcontinental discussions in 22 cities in the United States and Canada. Our authors then go on to forecast the kinds of research that remain to be done if we are to develop fruitful programs and strategies for our composition classrooms. There are 14 helpful appendixes and an extensive bibliography at the back of the book.

Jeanne W. Halpern and Sarah Liggett may well be mentioned in future histories as successors of the late Marshall McLuhan in bringing home to teachers of English the glad tidings about the electronic revolution. But as I have said in a number of public talks recently, I wonder who will become the Quintilian of the word processor. I am writing this Foreword on my new word processor, which was installed in my study at home in the very week that I finished reading the revised version of the Halpern-Liggett manuscript. After only a week of hands-on experience with this wondrous machine, I have acquired a keen sense of its potency and its potential—and the Halpern-Liggett study has confirmed what I sensed.

The Publication Committee of the CCCC Studies in Writing and Rhetoric series is pleased to present *Computers & Composing: How the New Technologies Are Changing Writing* to the academic world, not only because its message will be immensely useful to teachers but also because its publication puts the Conference on College Composition and Communication unequivocally in the vanguard of those educators who are not content to rest upon their past accomplishments but who want to draw up their syllabi for tomorrow.

Preface

SINCE THE GODS CAN, DEPENDING ON THEIR WHIMS, PLAGUE MANkind with curses of devious kinds, Zeus was surely within his rights when he created the first woman, Pandora. Graced with all the virtues the other Greek gods could bestow, she nevertheless had one quality that omniscient Zeus knew would be her undoing. For Pandora was placed on earth with a single possession, a box she was forbidden to open, and she was finally undone by curiosity. Lifting the cover of the box, she unleashed on humanity a multitude of plagues, and closing it, she trapped inside the only anodyne, hope.

We could not help wondering, as we wrote this book, whether some wily power was heaping upon us the gifts of a tantilizing idea and a herculean challenge, only to have us lift the lid on a subject that would become our undoing—and yours. Like Pandora's box, the new technology is fraught with possibilities for evil and good, and like Pandora, we have been impelled to open the box. But unlike Pandora, we have not closed the lid. This is a hopeful book.

We hope that you will find in these pages challenges—for research, for teaching, for using, perhaps, some of the new technologies we discuss. We hope that the colleagues and friends, too numerous to name, who have helped us develop this project will accept our thanks. And we hope, finally, that you enjoy *Computers & Composing*.

1

The New Technologies Are Changing Written Communication

WE LIVE IN AN AGE OF RAPID TECHNOLOGICAL CHANGE. IN THE popular press, such best sellers as Alvin Toffler's *Future Shock* and *The Third Wave* describe a world dominated by electronic information exchange. In academic publications—ranging from the *Harvard Business Review* to the *International Journal of Women's Studies* to *Today's Education*—dictation systems, computers, word processors, electronic mail, and telecommunication networks are the subjects of frequent articles. And in our own profession, conferences and journals underscore the impact of technological change on teaching English.

Nor is this a dramatically new phenomenon. For nearly two decades, technology has been gradually changing the way college graduates write. And it has elicited two reactions from those of us who teach composition. As Edmund Farrell noted in *English, Education, and the Electronic Revolution*, consistent interactions between man and media offer, on the one hand, "an ingenious means of further degrading human life," and, on the other, "the instrumentality for releasing the creative potential of each individual."[1] Similarly, Edward Corbett, writing in *College Composition and Communication*, pointed to two possibilities the new electronic media hold—for creating "passive automatons" or for developing committed, participating human beings.[2] The views of Farrell and Corbett, both published in 1967, anticipated what have in the ensuing years become two dramatically different responses to the new technology: repulsion and attraction.

Is "repulsion" too strong a word? Perhaps teachers in their English classrooms have simply equated television and computers with a vision of a brave new world which, without a stalwart system of defense, would lead to an Orwellian 1984. Interactive television and computerized filing systems, used by the government and private agencies to check on individual activities, certainly confirm this possibility. Or perhaps Marshall McLuhan's descriptions of the electronic revolution, which had become so obvious by the mid-sixties, coincided too closely with the reports of the Dartmouth Seminars which, by emphasizing the need for human values in the English classroom, dramatized the potentially dehumanizing effects of the new technology.[3] Whatever the reason, one line of response to the new technology has been resistance.

At the same time, however, a certain professional attraction for the new electronic media, an eagerness to see how they can be adapted to teaching, has emerged. Many teachers began using tape recorders to teach composition or to evaluate it; others presented BBC television productions of the Shakespeare plays and other filmed performances as subjects for writing; still others developed computer programs to improve spelling, grammar, and other writing skills in their classes or writing labs.[4] Such teachers have invited the new technology into their classrooms, intentionally narrowing the distance between their college courses and their students' lives.

If we have described the situation correctly, then the apparent polarity between the two prevailing professional views of technological change may not be as strongly charged as it appears. Proponents of both views attempt to connect the traditional, humanistic values associated with English to the lives of college students. Both emphasize learning. And both err, perhaps, in being too earnest: either in overemphasizing the negative effects of technological change on the quality of human life or in underestimating the consequences of an unconsidered surge toward change. The question is not whether to oppose or embrace the new technology but how to delineate productive responses to change.

Responding to Technological Change

In the October 1982 issue of *College English*, Lester Faigley and Thomas Miller showed that college educated people use a wide variety of media to compose: Over a quarter of the 200 people interviewed used computers to communicate in writing, and over a quarter regularly dictated their letters and reports.[5] "Whether for good or bad," Faigley and Miller concluded, "electronic technology will have long-range effects on the nature of writing."[6] What these effects are likely to be and how we, as a profession, can most appropriately respond to them is the question. It is clear, first, that we will have to define the elements of technological change most likely to affect the performance of our students. We will also have to formulate questions which address the most pervasive changes. And we will have to determine the kinds of research and classroom practice that will integrate the new technology into our theory and our pedagogy, while maintaining the humanistic values of our discipline.

The purpose of this book is to demonstrate how such tasks can be undertaken. We do not propose to map out in detail the great seas of technological change sweeping over written and oral communication; but we will chart the main currents which are likely to require the attention of English professionals. We do not propose to ask questions about each of the new electronic communication systems we identify; but we will select one important system for investigation and pose what we hope are appropriate questions about it. We do not propose to explore all of the research possibilities pertinent to the teaching of English literature, language, and composition; but we will show how research in composition can address the effects of technological change on teaching writing. We do not propose to restructure the content of freshman or advanced composition classes; but we will demonstrate how knowledge gained from research on technology can be incorporated in the teaching of writing, and how such teaching can be evaluated. We do not propose to look into the future of technological change and predict the composing processes our students will use in a global, postindustrial society; but we will identify topics which have emerged from our study and warrant further investigation. In other words, our goal is a modest one. We intend to show how researchers and teachers in our profession can begin to explore the effects of technological change on teaching writing.

Defining the Scope of the Problem

Toffler compares the widespread technological change occurring today with the nineteenth century change from an agrarian to an industrial society. The present change, however, is from an industrial to a postindustrial society, a society characterized by a white-collar work force heavily involved in information exchange and the manufacture of such products as computers and information systems, a society in which national boundaries blur and transnational corporations flourish.[7] Such a society depends on the productivity of the white-collar work force—executive and managerial, professional and technical, secretarial and clerical. Indeed, 50 percent of the national work force is now classified as having white-collar jobs, jobs in which people produce, exchange, prepare, and otherwise handle information.[8]

In the Faigley and Miller study, almost all of the respondents (193 of 197) said that they spend between 10 percent and 30 percent of their total work time producing written communications.[9] Other studies indicate that an even larger proportion of the work day is spent in oral communication of some kind.[10] The thrust of occupational change is toward white-collar personnel who communicate by writing and speaking. Since the media of communication are rapidly changing, it is incumbent on those of us who teach writing and speaking to understand the media most likely to affect the composing processes of our students.

Investigating the New Communication Systems

The new communication media with the most pervasive effect on college graduates are telecommunication networks, audio mail, electronic mail, word processors, and dictation systems. Each, while firmly grounded in the familiar, has changed in ways which affect written and oral processes and products.

In the past, and certainly in McLuhan's work, telecommunication networks were synonymous with TV screens watched by families in their living rooms. Newer telecommunication systems, however, are characterized by interactive features which allow a give-and-take between program personnel and viewers. At home, this interaction offers the opportunity for viewers to participate in live audience surveys, to answer quiz show questions, and to predict the plays and final scores of football, basketball, and baseball games.[11] In educational settings, interactive features allow instructors at a university to lecture, to present graphic materials, and to respond to questions from viewers at remote locations.[12] In business, industry, government, and the professions, interactive teleconferencing allows participants at conference sites in different cities, states, or countries to present information, solve problems, and make group decisions.[13] Teleconferencing of this kind may include two-way video and audio hookups among all sites, or one-way video from a central location and two-way audio connections between the central location and each site. In either case, however, costs are high and timing is critical because video transmission depends on satellite scheduling. For this reason, executives, managers, engineers, educators, and other professionals who participate in teleconferences often require special training in planning, in graphics presentations, and, if computers are included in the teleconference, in computer conferencing programs. A new profession has, in fact, grown up to provide educational training for those who participate in teleconferences.[14]

A second, more common electronic system, used in homes as well as offices, is audio mail. Audio mail links two familiar devices, telephones and electronic voice recorders, letting callers leave messages when the person called is not in. Since research shows that only half of interoffice calls successfully connect the caller with the person called, audio mail systems help foster communication.[15] The success of audio mail systems, however, depends on the caller's ability to plan and deliver a complete, coherent message that accomplishes the original purpose for calling. Users of audio mail systems have to overcome their reluctance to talk to a recorder and thereby avoid playing telephone tag—"This is Jones. Call me back."[16] Audio mail systems function best when "all the people in a working unit have the device and use it properly," according to Louis Mertes, Vice-President of Operations at the Continental Illinois Bank in Chicago.[17] In 1980, Continental installed over 300 audio mail devices and trained hundreds of personnel to use them effectively.

A third electronic system, or collection of systems, currently receiving attention is electronic mail. In the past, the most commonly known and frequently used form of electronic mail was the teletype, a system of electronic message transmission used between cities since the first such message—"What has God wrought?"—was transmitted between Washington and Baltimore in 1844. Another familiar version of electronic mail is facsimile transmission, or "fax," which allows the sender to put a letter or other graphic page into an electronic copying machine and have it scanned, translated into electronic impulses, sent over phone wires, and translated back into graphic form for the addressee, who may be in another office, another city, or another country. The newest version of electronic mail is based on computers; in these systems, a message is typed into a terminal, sent over phone wires, and translated by a receiving unit either into electronic form on a video screen or into printed form on paper. Employees of large corporations and federal units, for example, use computer-based electronic mail systems to communicate with each other at the office, between office and home, and between offices throughout the country.[18] To use such systems effectively, however, communicators must have a clear sense of audience and purpose; they must be able to create effective messages at the terminal, a practice often requiring special training in composing at the keyboard.[19]

The fourth new electronic system, which is often part of other systems such as electronic mail, is the word processor. Word processors resemble typewriters, but in addition to the familiar keyboard component, they contain computers, memories, and disk drives; they often have video screen and printer attachments; and they sometimes have modems, devices which can be attached to telephone units to connect word processors to communication networks and thus to other computers. Such telephone links allow users to "converse" over phone lines with others using word processors, to draw information from a central computing system, or to access information stored elsewhere in data banks. For instance, a biology professor may be preparing a research article at home on her word processor, which is connected by a telephone link to the central computer at the university. The professor can type in paragraphs as she composes them, dial up the university system for laboratory data stored in the main computer on campus, incorporate the data in her draft, print out a copy of the draft at home, and bring the computerized disk copy of the draft to the terminal in her office for additional work. Furthermore, she can, since the system in the biology department offers access to international computerized data banks, conduct a bibliographic search of articles and books on her topic, scanning abstracts on her video screen and printing out those she wants to use for reference. While such uses of word processing are becoming increasingly frequent in universities (especially in the sciences and social sciences), in government, and in business and industry, users of the new systems require technical training, generally provided by manufacturers or by company trainers. But those who use word processors for writing also have to learn to adapt the composing process they use in writing to word processing, which is not as easy as it might at first appear.[20]

A fifth new communication system now becoming increasingly important is dictation for word processing. Dictation, itself, has a long history. For centuries, scribes have translated spoken words into writing, as Tiro did when he took shorthand from Cicero, as Boswell did when he acted as Johnson's amanuensis, and as Dickens did in his job as court stenographer and later as parliamentary reporter for the London *Morning Chronicle*. Since the nineteenth century, stenographers have used the Pittman or Gregg shorthand systems to take dictation, and in the twentieth century, secretaries have transcribed either from shorthand or from recorded tapes. Each of these dictation systems has relied on a transcriber who knew the dictator, understood the context of the communication, and could check, correct, or add information as necessary. What is different in the new systems, which combine dictation with word processing, is the absence of personal contact between dictator and transcriptionist. The dictator can record a message wherever he or she happens to be—in an office, on a train, in a hotel—using a desk recorder, a pocket model, or a telephone. The taped message is then relayed to a round-the-clock word processing center and transcribed by a keyboard operator who may know nothing about the speaker, the context, or the relevant files. The transcriptionist prepares the letters, reports, or forms, usually has them printed, and returns the printed versions to the dictator, either for signing or for revision. Although such systems are flexible and efficient, they make new demands on the writer, especially the writer who expects to produce letters to be signed and sent immediately. To use the new systems effectively, such writers must be taught to dictate a message which is entirely self-contained and which, though spoken, looks as though it had been written for a reader.

As this brief introduction to several of the new electronic systems suggests, they share three characteristics. Each has emerged from an earlier, familiar mode of communication. Each is more efficient, more flexible, and less restricted by time or distance than its predecessor. And each requires special training for effective use. Furthermore, since the price of each of these systems is dropping as the technology improves and the demand rises, the new media will become an increasingly pervasive part of the work life and home life of college graduates. And these graduates will require new strategies and skills to use the systems effectively.

Such training can, of course, be provided by people outside the English profession, as is currently being demonstrated by consultants who prepare executives and managers for teleconferencing, by trainers who work for the manufacturers of word processors and dictation systems, and by in-house staff members who instruct personnel to use the new media on the job. But if teachers of English believe that they can, because of their insight into the composing process and their expertise in teaching composition, prepare students to be better writers, no matter what medium they use, then teachers will have to meet the challenge of the electronic revolution. The English profession will have to investigate the systems described above in careful detail, isolate the educational problems imposed by these systems, and come up with solutions which are theoretically justified and pedagogically sound.

Narrowing the Research Focus

Our professional response to the new technology thus far has been directed largely toward incorporating it into our pedagogical methodologies. We may videotape short instructional modules for use in the classroom or writing lab, use cassette recorders to evaluate student papers, and develop computerized instructional programs to help students improve their basic language skills. While it is useful to take advantage of electronic equipment in such ways, it is also essential that we examine the effects technology is having and will have on the composing processes of our students.

One way to do this is to examine how the new media are being integrated into the workplace, to see how they are being used, and to identify the problems writers face when they attempt to adapt what they have learned about pen-in-hand composing to the requirements of on-the-job technology. Since it would be impossible to explore all of the new media in one study, we have chosen to narrow our focus and examine in detail dictation/word processing systems. We have made this choice for several reasons. First, dictation systems are challenging, combining two cornerstones of our professional activities, speaking and writing. Second, there is ample literature on connections between speaking and writing, currently a subject of lively inquiry. And finally, the new dictation systems are likely to be even more widely used in the future, with such organizations as IBM and Bell Telephone Laboratories developing voice-to-word-processor systems which should, by the end of the century, be capable of transforming speech directly into print. For these three reasons, we decided to find out how and why the new dictation/word processing systems are currently being used.

By examining the literature and visiting sites throughout the country, we learned that dictation/word processing systems are changing on-the-job writing both quantitatively and qualitatively. Quantitatively, the new systems are beginning to dominate communication in government, business, industry, and the professions. The municipal government of Phoenix, Arizona, for example, installed a round-the-clock dictation/word processing network for city employees, from the mayor to the building inspectors, in 1978; less than two years later, over a third of the work at the Phoenix Word Processing Center originated from its dictation network.[21] Manufacturing Data Systems International, a medium-sized company employing about 700 people, converted to a mechanized system in 1976; by 1979, over half of the company's communications originated as dictation.[22] *Word Processing Systems* conducted a survey in 1980 to which 66 companies responded: "Sixty-four percent indicated that the use of dictation equipment has increased in their organizations during the past year and seventy percent say they see the use of dictation equipment increasing during the coming year."[23] Furthermore, professionals in various fields are rapidly integrating the new systems into their activities. Law firms are producing their legal communications and storing their administrative records on word processing systems; doctors in hospitals are using the new dictation systems for patient care records, research, and teaching; and accountants are composing their letters and reports on dictation systems.[24] As these examples suggest, conversion from writing to dictating resembles the change from ocean liners to jet planes in 1965; like the ocean liner, pen-in-hand writing is being replaced by faster, more cost-efficient methods which, like the jet, are likely to dominate the field by the end of the century.

Why are organizations installing the new systems at such a rapid rate? Dictation systems can reduce the time devoted to written communication up to 60 percent for short or routine messages and somewhat less for long or complex messages.[25] And these time savings translate into sizable long-term cost savings for organizations investing in the equipment.[26] In addition, the new dictation systems provide greater flexibility and efficiency to users, who can dictate wherever they are. Finally, dictation/word processing systems produce exceptionally attractive copy because they allow transcriptionists to format communications by using the appropriate function keys or programs and to change or correct communications before printing; final copy is usually flawless. Because of the advantages of time, cost, flexibility, and output quality, there is little question that the conversion to mechanized systems, which began in the 1970s, will transform the way college graduates write.

The new systems are, however, also changing writing qualitatively. According to Harvard research psychologist Howard Gardner, dictation compels writers to outline an entire argument in advance, thereby improving coherence and, at the same time, allowing dictators to capture fleeting thoughts or sequences of thought while dictating.[27] Furthermore, the new systems are transforming the very processes of speaking and writing. Walter Ong noted a similar transformation when he described the effect of writing on public oratory at the time of Aristotle: "Now, when you spoke . . . you were obliged to sound a little bit like writing quite regularly or perhaps even always. . . . You were expected to let your speech be colored by the way writing was or could be done. . . . After writing, oral speech was never the same."[28] The new dictation systems are causing similar changes in the way people speak *and* write.

But for people who use the new systems, such changes are not always easy. A survey of 2,000 randomly selected readers of *Modern Office Procedures* showed that while seven in 10 companies now have dictation/word processing systems, only one in three people who originate typewritten work actually uses the new systems.[29] If, as John Gould of IBM claims, writers can easily be trained to become effective dictators,[30] then why do so few writers use the new systems? Our exploratory research suggests that although writers can, indeed, learn the mechanics of dictation in a day, the actual process of speaking writing goes against the grain of their experience and education. They tend to associate the recursive process of writing with thinking, to rely on longhand drafts to turn their writer-based prose into reader-based prose, and to use longhand revision quite literally as re-envisioning. They have never learned to transfer these useful attitudes toward writing to dictating.

Our exploratory research on the new dictation/word processing systems has revealed something of a technological-educational dilemma. The systems are being introduced everywhere, but they are not being used efficiently because many writers, though trained in the technical process of equipment operation, are not able to adapt the composing process of writing to dictation. The enormous capital investments which organizations have made in the new systems put considerable pressure on personnel to use them; indeed, some organizations keep line-counts of systems use.[31] But on-the-job training, which emphasizes the technical process of dictation, does not help personnel to speak writing effectively. Such personnel need experienced teachers, teachers who understand the complexities of composing and who have a useful body of research to draw upon in teaching people to compose written documents orally.

Although we are not recommending that dictation become an important part of composition classes or that preparing students to succeed on their jobs be the central concern of our profession, our exploratory research does suggest that we, as teachers of writing, must provide students with composing strategies they can adapt to the media they are likely to encounter once they leave our classes. Deciding how to incorporate such strategies into our writing courses requires that we ask insightful questions about how writers compose on their jobs, that we answer these questions with careful research, that we draw on research in rhetoric and composition to devise new classroom practices, and that we evaluate and refine these practices to serve our students.

In the following chapters, we will show how we have used the information presented above to design a research study which describes how writers compose on the new systems, how this composing process differs from the composing process of pen-in-hand writing, and how understanding specific differences offers insights which can help us teach writing more effectively.

2

The New Systems Require New Composing Strategies

HOW DO WRITERS COMPOSE ON THE NEW COMMUNICATION SYStems? Does the composing process change when they dictate for word processing systems? If so, how do the new technical requirements affect the process of writing?

Answering these questions is likely to influence our research and teaching in several ways. It may prompt us to re-evaluate current models of the composing process in terms of their descriptive power. It may encourage us to incorporate into our models related research which has hitherto seemed tangential to our focus on written composing. It may lead us to reconsider the content of our writing courses which, for example, do not directly address the relationships between memory and writing, or speaking and writing. And it may tempt us to use in our classes technological innovations which may help students plan, write, and revise more effectively. Since research on technological change is likely to improve our theory and practice—and also, of course, help us prepare students more appropriately for the writing they will do in their careers—we propose in this chapter to examine closely one of the new communication systems and discuss our findings within the context of research on composing. More specifically, we will present the purpose, methods, results, discussion, and conclusions of our recent study of dictation/ word processing systems.

Purpose: Investigating Critical Features

Our exploratory research reported in chapter 1 showed that dictation/word processing systems were currently being used throughout the country, that the advantages of these systems assured even wider adoption in the future, but that many potential users were reluctant to dictate their communications on the new systems. Since these observations pointed toward a widening gulf between the technical requirements of on-the-job writing and the educational preparation writers receive, we conducted a descriptive field study to answer three questions:

1. How do successful users of the new dictation systems compose their communications?
2. What are the critical features of composing on the new systems, and how can these features be understood within the context of pen-in-hand composing?
3. What are the implications of our findings for teaching and research in composition?

To answer the first question, we conducted interviews with and collected materials from users and managers of the new systems, then analyzed the process successful dictators went through as they composed their communications. To answer the second question, we compared the results of our research with the process of composing described in recent literature in rhetoric and composition. And to answer the third question, we reviewed secondary materials and the results of our primary research, then formulated two sets of questions: one set intended to help teachers of freshman and advanced composition prepare their students for the new communication systems, and one set intended to stimulate further research.

We based our research on these assumptions: that it was possible to document and analyze the composing process of successful dictators; that the process we uncovered would differ in certain respects from the process of composing described in the literature of rhetoric and composition; that comparing the two processes would help teachers prepare students more effectively for whatever mode of communication they would use in the future; and that our results would also enhance the theoretical understanding of composing.

Methods: Analyzing Processes and Products

During our research, we conducted 28 structured interviews with users, managers, and operators of the new systems in business, industry, government, and the professions. Users of the new systems represented a wide range of careers. Among our interviewees were: an assistant deputy director of the U.S. Office of Education; a claims service representative of State Farm Insurance; a division director of the Indiana State Board of Health; a credit manager of Manufacturing Data Systems International; and a division manager of Michigan Bell Telephone. (For the complete list of interviewees, see appendix A.) We also collected interview forms on which users answered 11 questions including: What percent of your time is spent writing? What percent dictating? What process do you go through when you dictate? What specific skills do you need to dictate effectively? (For the complete list of questions, see appendix B.) Finally, we collected sets of notes, tapes, drafts, and final communications from users, plus instructional materials, user forms, and other documents from systems managers and word processing personnel. We then classified the communications produced using dictation systems, analyzed the processes dictators went through (as documented by their interviews and the materials we had collected), and prepared a descriptive chart which included all our findings on the composing process of dictation. (For the chart detailing the process of dictation, see appendix C.)

We will now illustrate the methods we used in conducting our descriptive research of on-the-job writers who use dictation systems by summarizing two representative case studies.

Case 1. On 26 June 1980, we conducted a structured interview with William Sonzogni, Director of Environmental Studies, in his office at the United States Great Lakes Basin Commission (GLBC). Sonzogni typically drafts journal articles, technical reports, memos, and other communications on the dictation/word processing system at GLBC. He uses dictation because: "I don't have to be at my desk"; "I can get something down quickly"; "I can dictate and revise at convenient times, see my progress, and have others comment on the draft"; and "I can cut down my natural wordiness when I see a chunk of text typed on draft sheets." As a result of our discussion and Sonzogni's answers on the structured interview form, we found that Sonzogni perceived his dictation process as follows:

1. Jot down some ideas;
2. Think about the ideas;
3. Consider questions or interests of my readers;
4. Revise and add details to my notes;
5. Develop an outline from the notes, rank ordering inclusions to move from what is most important to least important to my readers;
6. Assemble all necessary materials;
7. Dictate, rarely stopping to correct, but stopping between paragraphs to plan, sometimes adding afterthoughts to be inserted in the correct position when revising the draft: "Dictating helps my fluency";
8. Edit the first draft for conciseness, clarity, and sentence structure, "to make my writing short and to the point";
9. Ask others to respond to the corrected second draft, make appropriate changes, and have the changes incorporated in the final copy;
10. Proofread and correct the final copy; send.

When asked if he could document this process by describing a recent communication he had written, Sonzogni told us about a Summary of Actions he had completed to document a meeting of the GLBC Standing Committee on Research and Development; the Summary had been sent to 23 members of the Committee and to other interested parties the previous week. Sonzogni described the dictation in this way:

June 10
While attending the committee meeting, I jotted down a few notes; since I was very familiar with the subject matter, words and phrases were sufficient to trigger memory later.

June 11
In my office, I added a few details and scoped the thing out; I organized notes according to the concerns and sensitivities of readers on the standard mailing list.

June 12
In the grassy field next to the office parking lot, I dictated a rough draft from my outline and finished the dictation in my office. I rarely stopped to fix sentences but did stop between paragraphs to plan or add an afterthought for the secretary to insert. I gave the tape to our group secretary to transcribe, double-spaced on large draft sheets, on the word processor.

June 16
Over the weekend, I corrected the draft to cut out wordiness, then returned the corrected draft to the secretary and asked for a single-spaced second draft. She made the corrections at the word processor, checking off each correction in red pen on the original as she typed and asking me about unclear changes. She returned the second draft, single-spaced on standard pages, and I edited it.

June 17
I showed the revised draft to Lee Botts, Chairman of the Great Lakes Basin Commission, who made several suggestions which led to one substantive change and four stylistic changes. Later that day, the secretary entered the changes Lee Botts and I had made, gave me a final copy to proofread, inserted the appropriate mailing label list, and sent out the summary.

When we analyzed Sonzogni's notes, outline, tape, drafts, and final copy, we realized that he had a very clear perception of his planning process.[1] He was, however, unaware that during the actual dictation he averaged one tape stop every 5.5 words, not including directions to the transcriptionist; that he stopped repeatedly to plan phrases and words; and that whatever fluency he associated with dictation seemed to arise from his ability to articulate stock phrases rapidly. Similarly, Sonzogni's perception that he could "improve the conciseness, clarity, and sentence structure" of his communications as he revised and edited his drafts proved erroneous; the final copy was longer, was not much clearer (except in factual information), and was characterized by the same passive constructions, repetitions, and awkward and ambiguous phrasings that had appeared in the first draft. The only major stylistic or mechanical improvements on the final copy were made by the transcriptionist or by the outside reader. (For a segment of the edited first draft of the Summary, see appendix D; for a segment of the final copy, see appendix E.) Although several of the interviewees composed their drafts slightly differently than Sonzogni did, the basic process was the same: they planned and outlined carefully; paused repeatedly while dictating to plan sentences, phrases, and words; and revised their drafts, often with assistance from others, more for content than for style.

Case 2. On 6 June and 28 July 1980, we interviewed Prof. Bernard A. Galler, Editor-in-Chief, *The Annals of the History of Computing*, in his office at the Computing Center of the University of Michigan. After discussing the dictation and word processing equipment available at the Center and the uses he makes of the systems, we asked Galler to look over the structured interview form, ask any questions he had, and fill out the form; we then discussed his answers with him. From the discussion and the answers on the form, it became clear that Galler dictates frequently, usually producing first-time-final letters and emendations of stored texts or lists, and that he is unusually sensitive to the process he goes through, which he described as follows:

1. Consider audience, purpose, structure, and what the transcriptionist needs in directions and documentation;

2. Assemble relevant materials and files;

3. Think through the subject carefully, making a few notes;

4. Dictate at my desk recorder, making very clear distinctions between the text of the letter and the directions for the transcriptionist;

5. Replay the dictation tape "to face up to what it's like to listen to";

6. Correct the tape by dictating over errors: "I never leave a mistake on a tape";

7. Review the transcribed letters for errors and attach correction notes, though this is rarely necessary: "I occasionally let a minor awkward word or repetition go through, which differs from my habit in writing";

8. Instruct the transcriptionist to correct as necessary and send the letters.

Next, we asked Galler if he had at hand any recent samples of his dictated communications; he showed us copies of a series of first-time-final letters and emended lists for *The Annals* which he had completed a few days earlier. When we asked him to describe how he had produced these materials, he gave this narrative:

June 3
I came to the office in the evening, assembled the files pertaining to *The Annals*, and dictated this tape, which includes three letters and corrections for the stored contacts list for *The Annals*. I planned each unit of dictation from the files before me and made sure the tape of that unit had no errors before moving to the next unit.

June 4
The transcriptionist had put the finished letters, with envelopes, and a new printout of the corrected contacts list on my desk by 11:00 the next morning. I proofread, clipped correction notes to certain pages, signed, and returned all materials to the transcriptionist. She corrected and mailed the letters.

When we analyzed the tape and letters Galler had given us, we found that his dictation was characterized by repeated pauses (one every 6.9 words, not including directions), by directions to the transcriptionist, by corrections, and also by several changes made in the letters by the transcriptionist, of which neither she nor Galler were aware. (For a sample first-time-final letter, with all pauses marked, see appendix F.) Although several of our interviewees were less detailed than Galler in their descriptions of their composing processes, they all followed a similar pattern of composing.

Observations from the Galler case study, when combined with observations from studies of Sonzogni and others, allowed us to describe how successful users of the new systems compose, as we will explain in the following section.

Results: Composing on Dictation Systems

Our field study showed that approximately half of those who have access to dictation systems use them consistently; those who do not include a few old-timers who have always written in longhand and, more typically, relatively new staff members who think they cannot compose effectively by dictating—despite the fact that they have had on-the-job *technical* training in using dictation equipment.

Of the 28 people interviewed, 19 were responsible for composing internal and external written communications for their organizations; the rest were word processing managers or personnel. Of the 19 users, 10 consistently dictated their communications for transcription on the electronic systems provided by their organizations; three sometimes dictated and sometimes wrote their communications; and six always wrote in longhand, sometimes dictating their written drafts and sometimes giving the written versions to a secretary for typing. (Those who dictated written drafts felt they had to dictate, either because company policy encouraged using the systems or because they wanted to set an example for other staff members.) Though there was little correlation between a dictator's age and the use of dictation equipment, people in the highest positions always dictated their communications, claiming that dictating saved time and offered greater flexibility.[2] Our interview information thus confirmed the results of our exploratory research and provided personal explanations of why writers do and do not use the new systems.

Results which apply specifically to the first question we posed—"How do successful users of the new dictation systems compose their communications?"—are based on our analysis of information and materials collected from the 10 people who dictated consistently and whose finished products suggest that they dictate effectively. In general, our analysis showed what communications our interviewees composed and how they composed them.

Users of the new systems dictate four kinds of materials: drafts, first-time-final communications, forms, and records. No matter which option they choose, dictators follow the same underlying composing process: They plan in advance what they will say, they translate their plans into speech, and they usually review what they have said, either on tape or in print. This process would seem, in its general outline, to mirror the composing process in writing, especially in its repeated looping back and forth—between making a plan, translating it into spoken phrases, replaying the tape to review those phrases, then moving ahead with a new phrase. However, our results show that while certain features of the composing process of dictation resemble those of writing, other features differ dramatically.

Our research provides the following information about the distinctive features of the composing process in dictation.

1. *Advance planning in dictation includes three subprocesses*:
   - anticipating a dual audience, which means distinguishing between the needs of long-term (addressee) and short-term (transcriptionist) audiences;
   - choosing a dictation option—draft, first-time-final, form, or record—which is appropriate to the specific communication situation;
   - making mental notes, key-word outlines, or detailed outlines, based on assembled reference materials, to trigger memory of purpose, content, order, and detail during dictation.

2. *Translating advance plans into spoken text includes three subprocesses*:
   - ad hoc planning, which is signaled by frequent tape pauses—one every four to eight words—to decide on sentence development, phrasing, and wording; to avoid speech-related habits such as repetition and syntactic embedding; and to plan appropriate signals for the transcriptionist;
   - remembering, which includes recalling audience, purpose, content, and other items noted in key-word or expanded outlines, and also recalling syntactic and mechanical conventions of writing while speaking;
   - speaking clearly and distinguishing vocally the text of the message from directions for the transcriptionist.

3. *Reviewing on tape and in drafts requires several revision and editing skills:*
   - auditory review of tapes during translation, which depends on short-term memory and auditory scanning techniques and which allows dictators to move ahead with an idea, a sentence, or a phrase;
   - visual review of drafts, which is characterized by attention to content and mechanics rather than style, and sometimes by inattention to changes made by others;

- collaboration with others, including the transcriptionist and colleagues, and with the equipment to produce high-quality products.

Having summarized the results of our research, we will now identify the critical features of composing on the new systems and discuss them within the context of pen-in-hand composing.

Discussion: Identifying Critical Features

As Ong suggests when assessing the historic effects of technological change on consciousness, individuals adapt their thinking and behavior to the conditions imposed by the systems they use.[3] This was true when writing transformed speaking in the agora during classical times and when printing transformed the ordering and formatting of commonplace books during the Renaissance; it remains true today. Our results indicate that comparable transformations are occurring throughout the United States and, indeed, wherever technology is changing verbal communication.

Even though the current transformation is only beginning and our results do not allow us to generalize too broadly about its long-term effects on composing, we have identified seven critical features which characterize the composing process of those who dictate for word processing systems. These include:

- addressing dual audiences;
- using task-responsive advance planning strategies;
- making ad hoc plans;
- relying in special ways on long-term and short-term memory;
- incorporating oral delivery skills;
- using auditory as well as visual review procedures;
- collaborating with people and equipment throughout the composing process.

We will now address our second research question by examining these features of the dictation process within the context of current research on pen-in-hand composing. Our goals are two: to demonstrate that composing on the new systems includes cognitive processes which resemble but are, in certain important ways, different from those of writing, and also to explore the implications of our findings for teaching and research in composition.

We have selected as our general model of composing in writing that of Linda Flower and John Hayes. (For an illustration of the model, see appendix G.) While the Flower/Hayes model is derived from expository writing performed by college students and adult professionals, it provides a useful template against which to match our findings on transactional writing performed by those who dictate communications on their jobs. The model presents composing as a cognitive process with: (1) a specific task environment or message context; (2) a personal memory context; (3) three recursive activities—planning, translating, and reviewing; and (4) several specific subprocesses.[4] We will use this model, as well as other research in rhetoric and composition, to illuminate the critical features which characterize the process of those who compose on dictation/word processing systems.

Addressing Dual Audiences

Our research has shown that from advance planning through translating to reviewing, those who dictate for word processing keep in mind both the long-term audience who will read their communications and the short-term audience who will transcribe them. Consider, for example, this word-for-word transliteration of the beginning of the Galler tape which produced the first-time-final letter discussed above and displayed in appendix F. (Messages for the transcriptionist are in parentheses and italicized; words spelled out by the dictator are hyphenated.)

(Annals letter.) Professor Fritz Bauer *(B-a-u-e-r. He's on the editorial board so you should have an address for him on your Annals list.)* Dear Fritz. It was a great shock to me to learn about Klaus *(K-l-a-u-s)* Samelson *(S-a-m-e-l-s-o-n period)*. I remember very well the good times and the arguments that we had over ALGOL 58 *(that's all capitals A-L-G-O-L 58 period)*. I know especially that you and he were very close colleagues *(comma)*, and I am sure he will be greatly missed *(period paragraph)*.

As this transliteration shows, writers who dictate for word processing systems compose not only a complete, coherent message for the reader but also a string of short messages which will enable the transcriptionist to produce the communication. Dictation for word processing differs from other typical methods of transcription, such as transcription from stenography or from longhand, because keyboard operators receive their information aurally and know relatively little about the text they are typing or about its originator.[5] For instance, dictation to a stenographer or a personal secretary who knows the files and stylistic preferences of "the boss" is essentially a cooperative venture; the dictator can omit details and routine directions, focusing attention on the long-term audience and answering questions the secretary may ask during the dictation. On the other hand, pen-in-hand preparation is essentially self-paced and linear in terms of audience consideration; the writer composes for the long-term audience, then goes back and notes directions, draws arrows, and fixes handwriting, spelling, or punctuation for the short-term audience. As the Galler tape illustrates, however, dictation for word processing systems requires consistent attention to the needs of two audiences.

Although rhetoricians since the time of Aristotle have addressed themselves to audience analysis and adaptation, none has specifically discussed the audience switching which characterizes dictation for word processing. Perhaps the most relevant studies have been those associated with on-the-job writing, with register, and with dialogic and monologic discourse. In on-the-job writing, J. C. Mathes and Dwight Stevenson have identified three potential audiences for a specific communication: the primary audience, who makes decisions based on the communication; the secondary audience, who follows through on the basis of those decisions and with reference to the communication; and the tertiary audience, who transmits the message.[6] Although the transmitter is included largely to alert writers not to confuse tertiary with primary audiences, Mathes and Stevenson have clearly identified complications which may occur when writers do not distinguish between long-term and short-term audiences.

Studies associated with register and with the dialogic nature of spoken discourse and the monologic nature of written discourse also provide insight into the problem of dual audiences, although they do not address it directly. To cite one familiar example, Martin Joos in *The Five Clocks* quotes a recorded phone conversation about business matters in which he distinguishes the consultative style as one in which "the speaker supplies background information [and] . . . the addressee participates continuously."[7] The consultative style, which is clearly dialogic, is bounded on one side by the casual style, in which the participants in the dialogue are not strangers and may even be friends, offering a good deal of give-and-take as they converse, and, on the other side, by the formal style, in which "the crucial difference is that participation drops out"[8] and the speaker depends heavily on advance planning—of the entire discourse and of the paragraphs and sentences which comprise it.[9] Although the formal style, as Joos presents it, seems to describe the constraints under which dictators compose for both long-term and short-term audiences, most dictations intended for a long-term audience lean toward the consultative style (as though the dictators had anticipated the comments or questions a reader may have), while most dictated messages intended for the short-term audience lean toward the casual style. As John Schafer has pointed out, the dialogic aspect of speech seems to carry over into writing;[10] it is especially evident in writing which is dictated to be read by the long-term audience and in speech which is dictated to be heard by the short-term audience. Dictation, then, produces two concurrent dialogic monologues, both more or less consultative in style, but with one more closely approximating formal disourse and the other casual.

Since the dictator seems to anticipate that he will be bombarded with point-of-utterance decisions as he translates plans into language, he gives careful attention to audience needs in advance. Although much more research is needed on planning for and responding to dual audiences, our results suggest that students can best be prepared to face this challenge through rigorous training in audience adaptation and, especially, through deliberate instruction in the nature of spoken versus written discourse.

Using Task-Responsive Planning Strategies
   When a college freshman is given an essay exam to write in class, he has several options: Among them are drafting, fixing, and copying over; outlining (mentally or on paper) and writing; or writing straight through. When a busy credit manager has a short but important re-

port to dictate for her boss, she, too, has several options: She can dictate a draft and revise it; compose a first-time-final memo; adapt a computer-stored form she has used several times in the past; or record pertinent facts and figures and organize them later. Both the freshman and the manager are likely to consider how much time they have, what they know about the audience and the topic, and how important the assignment is—for a grade or a raise—and quickly decide how to proceed.

The difference is that the freshman can always shift gears. If the draft is not working, he can switch to an outline; if time grows short, he can hurry through the final copy. In dictation, however, an initial choice triggers a process which has its own procedures and constraints. Dictated drafts, first-time-final communications, forms, or records each call for somewhat different planning strategies, as we will now demonstrate.

Dictating drafts of complex communications usually requires deliberate planning. Indeed, engineers, managers, and professional writers who dictate long or complicated material seem to go through a planning process similar to the one described by Gardner: "Before I start to dictate, I prepare for writing just as I did before. I do the required reading, digest the material, and think about it; I then jot down an outline of a page or so, listing in order the major points I want to make. Then, instead of composing a legible draft on the typewriter, I begin talking into the machine as if I were lecturing to a small group of students."[11] Although our interviewees did not specifically identify invention heuristics, it was evident from their comments, planning notes, and outlines that they went through a process similar to Gardner's: They jotted down ideas that pertained to topic and audience, added facts and references they did not want to forget, gathered and looked through related materials, fiddled with a tentative order, and made their outlines before pushing the "record" button. Like Gardner, they dictated drafts *instead* of writing them for two reasons: because it is faster and because it allows a closer synchrony between thoughts and words.[12] They relied on drafts and redrafts to reconsider, reorder, and improve their work, usually with the help of others.

On the other hand, those who dictated drafts of *less* complex communications did it largely for personal convenience and did not use elaborate planning strategies. For example, George Heighway,

Director of Health Care Facilities at the Indiana State Board of Health, said that he composes all of his correspondence by drafting "because it's fast and very efficient."[13] For a letter like the Galler example described above, Heighway would do a quick draft, "drawing on what's in my files and what's in my head" and dictating "straight through." He would never review a tape, as Galler would. Instead, when the double-spaced blue paper draft came up from the word processing center, usually in about two hours, he would rely on his group secretary to "clean up my grammar and punctuation, so I can review for content only." Heighway uses the drafting option because it is compatible with his delegative method of management and his hectic schedule; it also seems to reflect his cognitive and certainly his personal style.

Dictating first-time-final communications calls for careful, though not always conscious, planning. Although dictators formulate mental plans or key-word outlines, they do not report using invention heuristics. In responding to a specific communication or assignment, they retrieve from long-term memory and from their files information triggered by the content and sender of the communication and, in some situations, by its tone. In creating original communications, such as Galler's letter, they use invention strategies linked to the context, purpose, and audience of the new communication. The writer of a first-time-final communication senses a need for writing within a given organizational context; explores his memory for information; collects relevant documentation; and decides on a style and tone likely to achieve the purpose of the communication vis-à-vis the intended reader—all of this rapidly and in an apparently unconscious way.

An interesting subclass of first-time-final communications which does suggest a conscious heuristic is patterned letters, such as responses to insurance claims or sales orders. Here, the dictator follows what is comparable to a simple story grammar and fills the slots with details relevant to the specific communication, details which, in fact, sometimes come from previously transcribed records. For example, Pamela Graves, Claims Service Specialist at State Farm Insurance, dictates standard patterned letters on claims adjustments using, among other sources, transcripts of recorded phone interviews with claimants and other parties.[14] In patterned letters, the general plan is stored in the dictator's memory; changes in the plan or details of the new content are written as planning notes. The memory-stored pattern thus acts as an effective heuristic for gathering and organizing new material—in a much less creative way than Kenneth Burke's pentad or the journalist's five "W's," but in a way that is entirely appropriate to routine communications.

Adapting form communications carries the patterning heuristic a step further. Writers select an appropriate form, usually from a notebook of letters, memos, and reports representing materials stored in the computer or on tapes or disks; next, they make notes of the original material to be inserted in the form; and finally, they dictate changes or insertions in line-by-line order, also attending to the stylistic and tonal constraints of the stored form. Sometimes this is a simple procedure. For example, when a personnel director writes to several interviewees to arrange plant trips, he simply follows the form letter and slots in dates, times, locations, and other information from planning notes, as he would in writing. But when an executive is preparing a periodic report or a lawyer is adapting a standard will form, the original material is sometimes so complex that she resorts to detailed outlines and may even attach complex original figures or addenda to the dictated tape. Whether the form adaptations are simple or complex, however, planning is essential because the dictation must match the stored form—in order, style, tense, and number—and, at the same time, incorporate necessary new information.

Dictating records is a common practice among doctors, credit managers, sales representatives, and others who consistently meet with many people every day. Those who dictate records generally follow a formulaic pattern to make sure they include all important information. For example, attorneys report using dictation equipment for records when working on wills, trusts, and other "future interest items." When an attorney meets with his client, he may ask a series of questions about the client's parents, brothers, sisters, children, personal life, and property. The next day, both client and lawyer may meet to go over the transcript of the previously recorded material and develop a new record, organized according to "The Problem," "The Facts," and "Procedures to Follow." From these records, the lawyer will draw up the appropriate document.[15]

This summary of the advance planning strategies writers use when they compose on dictation/word processing systems suggests two critical points about dictated composing. First, making the initial choice of which dictation option to use is uniquely important; in most cases, this choice determines planning strategies which affect the entire composing process. Although choosing the appropriate composing option in written composition is also important, relatively little research has been conducted on this subject. Lee Odell has noted that "different writing tasks make quite different demands on writers" in school and career contexts; C. H. Knoblauch, Thomas Pearsall, and others have shown that experienced pen-in-hand writers adapt their communications to purpose, audience, and other context-specific cues; and Janet Emig has shown that the general mode of production affects all stages of composing.[16] These observations clearly place the consideration of composing options in the task environment of the Flower and Hayes model. However, if students are to grasp this important feature of the task environment, they will have to learn enough about the new communication systems to understand the available composing options and the consequences of choosing one option over another.

Second, our research has shown that dictators plan the outlines and details of their communications in advance, using whatever procedure is appropriate to the task and to the cognitive style of the composer. The very process of dictation presses the dictator to prepare and plan as completely as possible before actually beginning to speak. Such planning may include using creative invention strategies, as in dictating drafts or some first-time-final communications. Or it may rely on formulaic heuristics, as in patterned letters, forms, and records, which are either internalized in the writer's memory or externalized on forms. (Although Gould has referred to a "spew" strategy in using dictation for drafting—a strategy not unlike Peter Elbow's free writing—we found little evidence of this technique in our research.)[17] Indeed, whether they relied on mental plans, key-word outlines, or more elaborate prefigurations, dictators planned most aspects of their communications in advance and usually did it quickly and effectively.

Perhaps the most compelling feature of our research on dictation is the prominent position of advance planning. In contrast, research in written composition has not always confirmed the importance of planning. Charles Stallard, for example, found that neither good nor randomly selected high school writers "showed any propensity for formal or informal planning of paragraphs or of the essay as a whole."[18] Furthermore, observations by Emig and Sondra Perl suggest that writing is more a process of ongoing discovery, reconsideration, and revision than of planning and translating into language.[19]

Recent evidence presented by Bonnie Meyer, however, supports the importance of planning for both writer and reader. Meyer identifies three functions of plans: a topical function, which helps a writer select and organize ideas; a highlighting function, which helps a writer indicate the relative importance of ideas; and an informing function, which helps the writer decide how to introduce new information in the context of previous knowledge.[20] Dictators use all three functions as they organize their ideas, format their messages, and clarify the context and purpose of their dictations in advance.[21]

Our results suggest that research on composing might well benefit from more deliberate attention to advance planning, not only as it pertains to invention but also as it pertains to deciding whether to invent or to follow an internalized pattern of presentation or to adapt a form communication. Our teaching should provide students with a wide range of advance planning strategies to use in different writing environments.

Making Ad Hoc Plans

The dictators we studied also planned consistently *during* dictation, pausing to consider sentences, phrases, and words. Although we were not present when the dictations occurred, relying instead on the tapes, drafts, and retrospective accounts of our interviewees, and although it is impossible to be sure whether the audible clicks on the tapes signal planning stops, reviews, or revisions, we can say that the pauses and clicks we heard generally preceded fluently dictated phrases; we assume that the pauses were used to plan those phrases. In this connection, Gould's laboratory research, which included close observation of subjects during dictation, led to the conclusion that ad hoc planning, as inferred primarily from pauses, accounted for up to two-thirds of composing time.[22] Available research, then, suggests that both advance planning and ad hoc planning account for much if not most of composing time in dictation.

Research on composing pen-in-hand writing does not consistently confirm this observation. Stallard did find that good high school writers stop more frequently than randomly selected writers, an observation also made by Perl in her work with college writers and English teachers.[23] While Stallard and Perl associate the pausing they observed with rereading what has been written and, especially in Perl's research, with revision, our investigation suggests that while pausing in dictation may be used to review what has been said, its main purpose is to plan the sentence or phrase, in a form appropriate to standard written English, which will carry out the writer's advance plan. This interpretation is confirmed by Ann Matsuhashi's analysis of pausing and planning in writing, which shows that pausing is closely associated with planning at the sentence level.[24] While a pause in dictation may, in some cases, trigger a new observation, on-the-job writers do not typically reconsider their ideas or discover new ones as they generate a text; according to their testimony and our observations, they plan their content in advance and their phrases as they move along.

Nor is this assessment incompatible with the Flower/Hayes model of writing. If we assume that planning activities occur not only at the beginning of the writing process but also during translating, as the model indicates, then the advance planning and ad hoc planning we observed support Flower and Hayes' results. Furthermore, if we take translating to mean specifically what Flower and Hayes say it is, "to transform [the writing plan] into acceptable written English . . . ,"[25] then our observations on the phrasal nature of translating plans into prose is confirmed. The ad hoc planning question in writing *and* dictating is: "How do I want to put this?"[26]

Our secondary research shows that pauses during composing have been interpreted in many ways—as opportunities to plan the next phrase, to think through a complicated sentence, to reconsider ideas, or to revise and edit the text that is being composed. Since the pausing which characterizes ad hoc planning is a critical feature of written and oral composing, the nature of such pauses warrants further research. When teaching oral composing, it is especially important to emphasize that pausing to turn advance plans into words is typical of the dictation process, as we will explain below in our discussion of memory.

Relying in Special Ways on Long-term and Short-term Memory

Long-term memory provides the writer with stored information about audience, topic, and optional forms of presentation, such as poems or stories or reports; with patterns or conventions of format, organization, syntax, style, spelling, and mechanics; and with some recollection of sentences or longer units that have already become part of the text being composed. Short-term memory allows the writer to retain what has just been thought, written, or said, a critical activity in discourse which lacks both a complete visual artifact and an interlocutor.

Our research shows that the complexity of composing for dictation encourages two distinct uses of *long-term memory*. On the one hand, dictators plumb their long-term memory *before* dictating for information on the topic, audience, and appropriate forms of written presentation (memo vs. letter; original vs. patterned vs. form); they carefully think through their entire communication; and they often jot down key words or outlines to trigger their memory as they dictate.

On the other hand, dictators also rely on long-term memory *during* dictation. Since they plan rapidly but thoroughly, they can elaborate in prose the plans they have jotted down, selecting sentence patterns, stylistic features, and mechanical conventions which, on the basis of their previous experience with reading and writing, seem appropriate to written discourse.[27] While, as we noted above, the style of dictated monologues may range from casual to formal, the dictator's frame of reference in the message intended for the long-term audience is the printed word. (In this connection, differences between the spoken code and the written code may explain not only the consistent pausing we noted but also the discrepancy between the impression dictators like Sonzogni have—that dictation improves fluency—and the fact that dictation is characterized not by rapid but by halting delivery.)

During dictation, long-term memory also appears to act as a retention bin for sentences that have just been formed. This function of long-term memory allows dictators to recall approximately what they have said or to give them a clear sense of how far back to go and what to listen for in an auditory tape review. Holding just-composed sentences in long-term memory also seems to allow dictators to avoid what Jerome Bruner called the "cognitive strain" of consciously attending to too many details, or what Carroll Arnold referred to as "the stress of the moment,"[28] in this case the moment of planning and uttering the next phrase. Finally, long-term memory may occasionally produce information overlooked in the advance planning memory search. When this occurs, dictators either rethink their plans and revise their tapes, or, more typically, jot down the new information and add it at the beginning or end of the tape, or in a hand-written note, so that the transcriptionist can insert it appropriately.

Dictators rely on *short-term memory* to recall just enough of the sentence they are composing to move ahead with the next phrase or sentence. Although dictators have several options for listening to what they have said before moving ahead, they seem less inclined at the moment of utterance to review a tape than to pause, recall the preceding phrase or two, plan, and produce a new phrase.

Research in composition has produced relatively little information on the uses of memory in composing.[29] This curious neglect may have several explanations. As Ong shows, the availability of printed material reduced the need to rely on memory for information and its transmission;[30] this transfer of focus may explain, to some extent, why memory receives less attention now than it did before writing and printing. David Olson carries this point a step further by suggesting that when authority is lodged in a printed text and meaning resides in the text, referring rather than remembering becomes the focus of schooling.[31] Corbett, in discussing the classical pentad, which included memory, offers another explanation: "after rhetoric came to be concerned mainly with written discourse, there was no further need to deal with memorizing."[32] But there is an important difference between memorizing as it was associated with delivery in classical rhetoric and memory as a system of storage and retrieval.

Research in psychology, and especially in schema theory, has addressed the systematic retrieval from long-term memory of information which pertains to a task at hand, and specifically to the reconstructive processes of memory in discourse.[33] Within this framework, the Flower/Hayes model incorporates the writer's long-term memory as a feature essential to planning in writing. Although Flower and Hayes say relatively little about the process in their discussion of the model, they do observe that writers draw on knowledge about topic, audience, and patterns appropriate to a given performance when they plan, and that they draw on information about written sentence patterns when they translate their plans into prose.[34] Furthermore, in discussing the dynamics of composing, Flower and Hayes refer to conscious or unconscious choices writers make during the process of composing to avoid taxing the short-term memory, such as relying on original and stereotypic plans.[35] Not only do our results confirm the uses of memory distinguished by Flower and Hayes, but they also lead us to make two observations: that the pressure to deliver not one but two concurrent monologues forces the dictator to reduce the complexity of oral composing by transferring, insofar as possible, memory searches and all planning except sentence formulation to the beginning of the composing process; and that the pressure to compose aloud makes the dictator unusually dependent on long-term memory.

Our results suggest that students should be taught to pay conscious attention to memory as they learn and as they write—not as though it were a muscle to be exercised, but a strategy to be used in composing. Our results also suggest the need for more specific information on how experienced writers use memory during composing and how strategies for drawing on long-term and short-term memory affect recursiveness.

Incorporating Oral Delivery Skills

Oral delivery is a complex and extremely important feature of dictated writing. With its "uhms," breaths, throat clears, pauses, clicks, and two threads of discourse, a dictation tape represents a self-consciousness about oral delivery which distinguishes it from both conversation and public speaking, though it includes features of each. Like conversation, dictated speech seems to respond to questions, imagined or anticipated, and to proceed despite or around interruptions; like public speaking, it is planned, sometimes articulate, and generally not characterized by the informality of everyday speech. Unusual though they certainly are, dictated tapes represent many features we associate with literate oral delivery.

The grammatical facility of our interviewees is probably the result of former schooling; most had had at least four years of college. Delivery skills, on the other hand, seem to have resulted from in-house training. The directions that writers receive from manufacturers of dictation/word processing systems or from in-house trainers generally contain advice on how to enunciate clearly, at a moderate speed, and with regard for the listener.[36] Experienced dictators do these things, and dictators who get especially good copy back from word processing centers do them very well.

But most on-the-job writers did not learn to speak effectively in their English classes. Although instruction in English has traditionally been intended to develop reading, writing, listening, and speaking abilities,[37] the fourth member of this quartet generally drops out by tenth grade, when many high schools introduce elective speech or public speaking courses; there is little planned oral presentation in high school or college English classes, except by the teacher.

However, our profession has, especially in the last two decades, begun to investigate oral discourse, largely because of important psychological and neurological research about relationships between the cognitive processes of thinking, speaking, and writing; because of studies on improving writing through speaking; and because of investigations on the needs of college graduates to speak effectively on their jobs. Momentum for these studies has come from primary research by Lev Vygotsky, Aleksandr Luria, and James Gibson on the nature of language acquisition and performance.[38] Similarly, inquiries in English education, such as those of James Moffett and Robert Zoellner, have addressed language development, oral discourse, and pedagogy.[39] A third line of inquiry—based largely on the needs of on-the-job writers to summarize reports briefly and effectively, to conduct meetings expeditiously, and to use dictation and teleconferencing systems efficiently—is reflected in work by Marie Flatley and Gretchen Vik and suggests the need for continuing research on oral delivery.[40]

At the moment, however, our profession seems to be divided on the usefulness of developing writing and speaking as complementary verbal abilities. On the one hand, Emig, Nancy Sommers, and others counterpose writing and speaking, showing that writing is a unique process, eminently suited to learning, and proposing that much of what is ill-conceived in the teaching of writing issues from its oratorical heritage.[41] On the other hand, most of the authors represented in *Exploring Speaking-Writing Relationships: Connections and Contrasts* view the two language production skills not only as complementary but as intimately related in the development of thinking, learning, and the mastery of verbal performance. Our own results not only confirm the latter view but also show that without refined oral delivery skills, students who write effectively in college classes may not communicate effectively in their careers. As Barry Kroll indicates, practice in both modes is likely to improve overall verbal performance.[42]

In terms of teaching and research, our findings suggest that providing opportunities to improve oral skills in the composition classroom will prepare students for using the new communication systems effectively and may improve their writing. However, since most of the research on relationships between speaking and writing has been theoretical or descriptive, rigorous experimental studies are needed to test the assumption that practice in speaking improves writing.

Using Auditory as Well as Visual Review Procedures

Because reviewing, revising, and editing on the new dictation systems can be auditory and/or visual, dictators adapt their procedures to the dictation options they have chosen. Those who dictate *drafts* use auditory review mainly to plan what they will say next; like pen-in-hand writers, they use draft sheets to rethink, restructure, and refine what they have said. And like pen-in-hand writers, they adapt their visual review strategies to the purpose of the communication. For noncomplex communications, they consistently attend to factual content rather than style, even though, like Sonzogni, they think of revising as polishing. Those who draft more complex materials, such as technical reports, also focus on content, but they consciously attend to organization, focus, cohesion, formatting, and phrasing, switching paragraphs, and adding transitions to improve content and style. Those who dictate drafts of what we would call professional writing—articles, chapters, books—use printouts as first drafts, attending to content, organization, and style, and doing "everything writers do to discover and develop what they have to say."[43]

Those who dictate *first-time-final communications*, on the other hand, rely heavily on auditory review, not only to "glance back" over what they have said before they move ahead but to revise and edit their communications on tape; they use visual review only to correct finished copy. (Occasionally, they reconsider and revise first-time-final messages once they see them in print, but more typically they let less-than-polished prose slip through to save time.) Writers who use dictation systems for adapting *stored form communications* combine or use either auditory or visual review: For simple form messages, they rely on auditory review and ask the transcriptionist or word processing proofreader to check the copy; for complex form reports, they use auditory and visual review. Those who produce *records* typically do not review, revise, or edit, except, perhaps, when they call up the record for later use.

Options for using different review procedures for different occasions are enhanced by the special features dictation systems offer. Audible fast-forward scans, available on equipment with speed control features, allow writers to review an entire text rapidly, as they would glance through the pages they have written to get an overview, to reconsider their direction, to revise large chunks of text, or to edit.[44] Replay and tape-over features allow dictators with portable, desk, or phone recorders to review, revise, and edit tapes quickly. Video screens allow them to see the transcript before it is actually printed and make changes. (Although this is not a typical procedure, it occurs when dictators have access to communications as they are being keyboarded and before they are printed; video screen review occurs mainly when tapes are transcribed in word processing centers which serve a group or unit rather than an entire organization.)[45] And finally, the revision capabilities of word processors allow for a fast sequence of corrections or redrafts, enabling writers to see immediately how the changes they have made look in print. Our own experience with drafting, revising, and shortening book reviews and book chapters to meet space requirements suggests that there is no more efficient way to polish a text than with word processing.

In general, then, the capabilities of dictation/word processing systems allow writers unaccustomed flexibility in deciding how they will revise and edit their writing. The strategies they use depend on the dictation options they choose, the purposes of their communications, and the importance and pressures associated with the kinds of writing they do.

Recent research on revision in on-the-job writing confirms our findings. Gould, in his laboratory studies of on-the-job writers who dictated and wrote one-page, first-time-final letters, found that whether dictating or writing, the subjects "made few changes, either while composing or in subsequent proof-editing," and that the changes they did make while composing were "local" rather than "global," that is, contiguous or close to the portion of spoken or written text they were producing.[46] Similarly, Barrie Van Dyke, in her interview-survey of 80 bank executives, found that they chose to dictate simple letters to clients or memoranda to bank personnel and reviewed these only for typographical or mechanical errors.[47] Van Dyke also found that the executives drafted more complex communications, both external and internal, and that the more important or involved the assignment, the more carefully and deliberately they revised. For example, special reports which resulted in major decisions for the bank were revised in multiple drafts for organization, focus, impact, and sometimes length and overall presentation. The salient point in these investigations and in our own is this: The dictation option a writer chooses, plus the purpose and the importance of the specific communication, determines revision strategies.

In terms of current research in rhetoric and composition, we would therefore agree with Donald Murray: "The evidence we have [on revision] is restricted to a very few forms of writing."[48] The evidence Murray presents, which points to revision as a process of discovery, is based on a wealth of documentation from poets, novelists, dramatists, and essayists. The evidence Sommers presents, which shows that revision occurs "continually throughout the writing of a work," is based on studies of experienced journalists, editors, and academicians.[49] The evidence Perl presents, which portrays composing as a backward-moving action of a retrospective structuring, is based on studies of college students and English teachers.[50] As Odell has noted, understanding how those who compose business letters and technical reports review their work is likely to complement the present understanding of revision.[51]

If we view our research and that of Gould and Van Dyke within the Flower/Hayes model, we find justification for the position that reviewing strategies are context- and task-dependent. Flower and Hayes distinguish clearly between editing, which interrupts a plan for translating ideas into prose in order to fix what has just been produced, and revising, which occurs after translating, when writers can "devote a period of time to systematic examination and improvement of the text."[52] Our own research suggests that while both activities occur in dictated texts, they do not necessarily occur in the same texts. Writers who dictate drafts use auditory review mainly to plan the next stretch of discourse and occasionally to correct; more often they revise and edit their drafts on paper, the amount of attention they pay to revision depending on the purpose and importance of the text—to the writer and/or to the organization. By contrast, first-time-final writers listen, edit, and if they are, like Galler, unusually conscientious, revise on tape; but as Gould and Van Dyke have noted, they are more inclined to correction than revision.[53]

Our results suggest, first, that teachers would be wise to alert students to the full range of reviewing, revising, and editing strategies they can use for different occasions, rather than to emphasize only those which seem most appropriate to professional writers. Our results also suggest the possibility of using dictation equipment in the classroom to help students learn a full range of reviewing, revising, and editing strategies, a procedure likely to be especially effective with students whose composing style is characterized by an impatience to get their assignments done, students who might not typically review or revise their work but might be attracted to concentrate on their texts through auditory review. Finally, our results suggest that researchers should pay much closer attention to the reviewing strategies used by busy writers who compose wherever and whenever they can. Although, as our own project has shown, isolating reviewing strategies is no easy task, it is likely to bring useful rewards—for our teaching, our theory, and our research methodology.

Collaborating with People and Equipment Throughout the Composing Process

As all of our interviews and examinations of tapes and transcripts have shown, the transcriptionist is an essential link in the system of message production.[54] Not only does she (we encountered no "he") affect the production of the message by being its short-term audience, but she may actually change the message. In drafting, the transcriptionist often writes marginal questions about a dictation and, if she works for a group, adds factual file information such as dates, places, and names; furthermore, other staff members are often involved in improving or actually collaborating on a text. In preparing first-time-final messages, the transcriptionist makes subtle, sometimes unnoticed changes. Galler, for example, the interviewee most conscious of his entire composing process, did not notice that the transcriptionist had made three small, positive changes in the short first-time-final letter he dictated. Although collaboration has never been an unusual practice in large organizations, it seems far more prevalent now because of the ease and speed of dictated drafting, word processing revision, and rapid printing and copying.

This brings us to the extraordinary interdependence of people and machines in the new communication systems. Ong has, in his detailed description of the talked book, illustrated the "superimpositions of electronic orality, writing, and print on or through one another."[55] We have observed similar interdependences in following, for example, the Sonzogni manuscript—from notes to outline to speech to keyboarding to printing to pen-in-hand revising to keyboarding to copying to outside revising to editing to keyboarding to correcting to copying to list processing to mailing. And there are even more possibilities—if we include computerized storage and retrieval systems, text-editing and graphic design programs, and interactive videotext systems.[56] No matter how new or complex the technology, writers consistently interact with it as they compose.

Writers who dictate are as aware of the media and the muscles they use as other writers are of paper, pen, hand, and eye. Dictators devise new strategies to focus on notes with their eyes, even as they translate plans into words with their lips, press buttons with their fingers, and review taped phrases with their ears. They anticipate how a message will sound through the transcriptionist's earphones, how it will look on a screen, in a printout, in a memo. Those who dictate their writing are, in fact, intimately involved in a physical and mental collaboration with the equipment they use. "Not only," as Ong notes, "is there talking, writing, and printing going on but each one of these is being carried on with a conscious reference to the other."[57] The more readily writers adjust their experience with composing to this intense interaction with the media they are using, the freer they become to use the systems creatively—just as children who have learned *how* to write become freer to concentrate on *what* to write, and faculty members who have learned how to use word processing keyboards become freer to invent, type in, revise, and hone their ideas.

Collaboration with people and equipment is clearly part of the task environment, which, according to Flower and Hayes, "includes everything outside the writer's skin that influences the performance of the task."[58] When George Heighway of the Indiana State Board of Health, for example, dictates the draft of a letter and does not review it before having it transcribed, he is relying on certain features of the task environment: that the draft will be transcribed and printed at the word processing center; that his secretary will "fix" the grammar, spelling, and details; that he'll be able to scan and revise for content; that the transcriptionist will enter all corrections on the word processor, print the complete text on letterhead, and return the finished letter for signing. Drafting, which is the composing option Heighway generally chooses, implies a specific task environment, an interaction with people and equipment that occurs only because Heighway is dictating a draft for word processing.

To some extent, research and teaching in composition have introduced students to collaboration at different stages of the composing process. Several studies have shown the effectiveness of collaboration in planning,[59] even while acknowledging that, as John Dixon has noted, "To write . . . is to move from social and shared work to an opportunity for private and individual work."[60] Furthermore, several collaborative planning strategies overlap into the translation-into-writing stage, especially in work with inexperienced writers.[61] But it is in the reviewing stage that teachers have paid most attention to collaborative efforts, especially in peer evaluation.[62] How to pull these relatively discrete applications of collaboration in writing together and integrate them with the notion of interactive media is an open question. But we believe that, in their classes and in their research, teachers will have to make new connections between the individual process of composing on paper and the collaborative process of composing on the new communication systems.

Conclusions: Implications for Teaching and Research

We posed a third question at the outset of this study: "What are the implications of our findings for teaching and research in composition?" Examination of our research within the framework of the Flower/Hayes model and other literature in rhetoric and composition suggests several important differences between composing in writing and composing on dictation/word processing systems. Most important are differences prompted by the task environment. Attending to a dual audience, choosing the appropriate dictation strategy, manipulating the equipment, speaking writing, and having no visual artifact to review: These constraints dramatically change the context of planning, translating, and reviewing. The task environment seems, on the surface at least, to press the writer toward a more linear, less recursive composing process. Those who dictate seem to plan what they will say and sketch an outline of how they will say it in advance, and to rely on ad hoc plans to solve speaking/writing problems as they move along. How priorities are assigned to the subprocesses of composing in dictation is unclear, largely because the stops, starts, and tape clicks give no consistent indication of why they occur when they occur. But it is clear that the process of composing on the new systems warrants further attention by our profession.

To determine the specific implications of our investigation for teaching and research in composition, we have developed two sets of questions, one of which addresses teaching and the other research.

Questions about Teaching

Although teachers cannot anticipate all of the rapidly changing features on the technological landscape, they can provide a map which will help students understand the lay of the land and prepare for some of the swamps and precipices they will encounter. Teachers can best serve students by placing writing within the broad framework of expressive, transactional, and poetic discourse described by Britton et al., in which "transactional" includes "those uses of language where the writer, operating in a participant role, seeks . . . outcomes in the actual world."[63] Considerations of current postcollege transactional writing lead us to ask:

- What is this "actual world"? What task environments does it offer writers? How can teachers introduce students to these environments?

- How can teachers introduce audience adaptation strategies which focus attention not only on content but also on stylistic considerations such as critical differences between speaking and writing and similarities between dialogic and monologic discourse?

- How can teachers provide opportunities for students to plan communications in a variety of ways, using heuristic strategies which encourage invention and also using more patterned or formulaic responses to assignments?

- How can teachers develop in students a sensitivity to and memory of the visual, syntactic, and mechanical conventions of written prose which they can draw on as they speak written texts?

- How can teachers help students develop oral skills which are likely to improve both speaking and writing?

- How can teachers introduce a wide range of auditory and visual reviewing strategies?

- How can teachers include collaboration—with people and with equipment—in their composition classes?

Although such questions may seem difficult, answering them is likely to depend largely on ingenuity—in bending the strategies now used and the subject matter now taught in slightly different directions. In the next chapter, we will show how these questions can be addressed in freshman and advanced composition classes.

Questions for Research

Lee Odell and Dixie Goswami have shown that examining the writing adults do as a regular part of their daily work provides insight into the choices they make and the processes they use.[64] Although our research has helped to define the conceptual processes involved in on-the-job writing, it has also raised many questions that require further exploration—not only about the effects of dictation/word processing systems on writing, but also about the adequacy of our current research models in light of widespread technological change. Research questions prompted by our study include:

- How is the choice of a dictation option—an important feature of the task environment of composing on the new systems—related to the purpose of a document and the cognitive style of the composer?

- Does response to the needs of multiple audiences in protocol analysis offer insight into the nature of audience adaptation in composing? If so, how can researchers use the large body of protocol analysis transcripts to better understand audience adaptation, especially as it pertains to register, spoken vs. written syntax, and monologic/dialogic patterns of discourse?

- In what ways are current invention heuristics, such as tagmemics, appropriate to the tasks of on-the-job writers, especially those who use electronic systems? In what situations is the discovery of ideas and data so routine as to require little or no invention?

- What resources from cognitive psychology can provide clearer insights into the variety of planning strategies required for different kinds of transactional writing and different discourse situations?

- How do writers draw on long-term and short-term memory in composing? How do the strategies they use differ according to the communications they are composing and the media they are using?

- How can improving oral delivery skills enhance writing?

- What pressures and constraints affect revision and editing in composing on the new media?

- How does recursiveness in pen-in-hand composing differ from recursiveness in composing with electronic media?

- How can the new technology be used most effectively to help students plan, translate, and review their written work?

- In what ways can classical rhetoric, with its attention to the arts of invention, arrangement, style, memory, and delivery, be integrated with the cognitive process model of composing?[65]

- How can we develop heuristics which satisfy what Janice Lauer calls a "metatheory of heuristic procedures" by being transcendent, flexible, and generative enough to incorporate the changing features of composing on new communication systems?[66]

Big questions, these, but ones worthy of continued attention, as we will show in our last chapter when we return to them within the context of global technological change.

Responding to Change

In the most general sense, the considerations that have emerged in our research are old and new, old in their general outlines and new in their specific features. They are echoed in ancient fears that writing would not enhance but rather would reduce man's ability to think, and in later forebodings that literacy would alter the conduct of government, business, and religion—as indeed it has.[67] But more recent, specific concerns associated with the effects of technology on human behavior emerged in the 1960s, partly as a result of television and computerized technology, and partly as a result of McLuhan's dramatic analysis of their potential effect on people's lives.

The communication systems addressed in our research did not exist in 1967, when Farrell wrote *English, Education, and the Electronic Revolution* or when Corbett wrote "What Is Being Revived?" in *College Composition and Communication*. But Corbett's conclusion in that article still deserves attention:

> If Marshall McLuhan's apocalyptic pronouncements about our imploding electronic world are true, then we shall have to take a good hard look at our curricula, our textbooks, and our teaching methods. In that process of reassessment, we might find that some of McLuhan's insights will be helpful to us in fashioning a rhetoric that is relevant to our age. The rhetorics of the past have all been concerned with the composition of a discursive, uninterrupted monologue. What we seem to need now is a rhetoric of the process rather than of the product, a rhetoric to guide us in forming the mosaic structure of so much of our policy-setting, information-dispensing, attitude-forming discourse today—the brain-picking sessions, the symposia, and panel-discussion, the interview—in short, a rhetoric of the stop-and-go, give-and-take dialogue, or should we say the "polylogue"?

If the same kind of topnotch people who turned their attention in the post-war years to the development of semantics, linguistics, and literary criticism apply their talents to the development of rhetorical theory and practice, then we are likely to have a vigorous revival of rhetoric, and the revival will increase its chances of creating a valuable legacy for the profession.[68]

Whether the new electronic media and McLuhan's pronouncements about them actually *caused* the shift in perspective that Corbett presaged is uncertain; but that we have, indeed, moved toward a "rhetoric of process" is clear. Such a rhetoric can, however, only become "a valuable legacy for the profession" if it is flexible enough to accommodate changes imposed by the environment in which writing occurs. Our research suggests that conceiving of writing as a cognitive process offers innumerable possibilities for responding, in our teaching and our research, to the technology that surrounds us, as we will show in the next two chapters.

3

Teachers Can Use Research about the New Systems in Freshman and Advanced Composition Classes

OUR INTERVIEWS WITH ON-THE-JOB WRITERS, OUR DIRECT OBSERvations of the new communication technologies, and our secondary research convince us that the workplace and the classroom are like two continents, gradually drifting farther apart. In an effort to make connections between these two writing environments, we will demonstrate in this chapter how teachers can translate the conclusions drawn from our research into successful teaching. Although the pedagogical practices we will discuss have been used successfully in freshman and professionally oriented advanced composition classes, we will emphasize not the practices but the process of transforming research into effective teaching.

We will begin by formulating a general course objective based on the descriptive research reported in chapter 2. At the most general level, the objective is:

> To introduce students to the new communication systems and help them adapt the process of pen-in-hand composing to the challenges of the new systems.

From this general objective, we will derive specific teaching goals for freshman and advanced composition courses. Since such goals will differ according to class level, we will adopt Ross Winterowd's useful distinction between transferable and local skills[1] in developing the two sets of goals. For freshman composition courses, we will emphasize transferable skills, under which Winterowd includes such features as developing a sense of audience, syntactic fluency, and control of diction. For advanced composition courses, such as business, technical, and professional writing, we will also include local skills, under which Winterowd includes knowledge of special forms, styles, and vocabularies. Although our specific teaching goals at each level will differ, both sets will address the pedagogical questions raised in chapter 2.

In the following discussion, then, we intend to show how teaching goals, derived from our general objective of introducing and preparing students to use the new systems, can be incorporated in composition courses. Because many of these goals may be close to or even the same as those which teachers traditionally address in composition classes, we will emphasize only their *distinctive applications* in preparing students for technological change. The first section illustrates the adaptation of specific teaching goals to freshman composition, presents the development and use of a performance objective, and ends with a short subjective evaluation. The second section presents a similar approach for professionally oriented advanced composition courses, again ending with a performance objective and an assignment derived from it. The third section demonstrates how experimental research can be used to test the effectiveness of teaching.

Defining Teaching Goals to Introduce the New Systems in Freshman Composition Classes

The strongest and most distinctive influence of the new media on the composing process is the task environment, which affects decisions about planning, writing, and revising. Students should understand the wide range of task environments they may encounter and be prepared to adapt their composing processes to the media they will be using—possibly in college and certainly in their post-college careers. Similarly, teachers should realize that the goals we will now discuss are intended not to change the basic curriculum of freshman composition but to increase its power to address the effects of technological change on writing.

In this section, then, we will discuss seven specific teaching goals appropriate to freshman composition:

- introducing students to the new systems through interviewing, reading, discussing, and writing;
- providing opportunities for students to address different audiences through speaking and writing and to identify differences between the two modes of language production;
- encouraging alternative planning strategies for different kinds of assignments, strategies ranging from formal invention heuristics to formulaic patterns of discourse;
- developing a tutored sensitivity to the visual, syntactic, and mechanical conventions of writing through reading;
- developing oral skills;
- developing a variety of auditory and visual reviewing strategies;
- providing frequent opportunities for collaboration.

We will discuss these goals within the context of the task environment and its effects on planning, translating plans into writing, and reviewing.

Task Environment

In preparing students to understand and respond to the unusual task environments created by the new media, teachers should introduce the wide range of technologies now being used for written and oral communication. In so doing, they should emphasize considerations of audience and differences between speaking and writing.

Introducing students to the new systems through interviewing, reading, discussing, and writing. To plan effectively for composing on the new systems, students must first understand the effects of these systems on the task environment of composing. As we noted in our discussion of dictation/word processing systems, students should learn enough about the new technology to understand the composing decisions they will have to make when planning their messages.

Since teachers cannot be expected to be experts on the kaleidoscopic range of electronic media, they can ask their students to explore with them the world of on-the-job composing through primary and secondary research and to share their findings in class. For example, teachers who suggest "communication technology" as a topic for a research paper can involve students in original research projects. When time and resources allow, they can encourage students to use methods similar to the ones we used when we visited on-the-job writers and examined secondary sources—conducting taped interviews with vendors, managers, and users of the new systems; seeing how the systems work; and reading articles in popular and professional publications. When they conduct research about the new systems, students can be encouraged to use or read about the media they are investigating. At some colleges and universities, for example, students may have access to computer-based retrieval systems, such as ABI/INFORM or Management Contents, to locate articles describing the new technologies. Students will also benefit from reading anthologies which contain sections on the new communications media.[2] As McLuhan has noted: "The method of our time is to use not a single but multiple models for exploration."[3]

To conduct such research, students have to be taught to develop good questions and find information which shows how the new media affect writing. As June Ferrill suggests, this may require class discussion which allows students to target appropriate goals for their projects, decide how audiences will use the information, and plan the form in which it will be presented to teachers, class members, and perhaps others.[4]

Providing opportunities for students to address different audiences through speaking and writing and to identify differences between the two modes of language production. Learning about the new systems will show students that different media require different audience considerations: Electronic mail is generally addressed to an audience of one or to a homogenous group; dictation/word processing systems have dual audiences; teleconferencing and teletext networks have multiple, sometimes heterogeneous audiences. Furthermore, such systems may require either speaking or writing or a combination of both. Student investigation of the new communication technology is likely to bring audience considerations to the forefront of class discussion. Giving students opportunities to present their findings to others will allow them to adapt their speaking and writing skills for different audiences. But teachers can also lead students beyond these specific experiences. As Olson explains, "Writing is not merely speech written down . . . it involves a substantially different, more specialized language code tied to a more specialized knowledge system."[5] Whether the text produced so far is oral or written, knowledge of the linguistic conventions of speaking and writing strongly affects the composing process. Although teachers know this, they do not typically emphasize differences between speaking and writing in their classes. By having students transcribe the research interviews they taped, convert the transcripts of speech into written prose, and categorize and discuss the kinds of editing changes they made, teachers can sensitize students to consistent differences between speaking and writing.[6]

In general, to prepare students for the task environment of the new systems, teachers can incorporate three activities in their classes: a general introduction to communication technology, assignments that require adaptations for various audiences, and discussions of the differences between speaking and writing.

Planning

In the new systems, choosing an appropriate planning strategy is linked not only to topic, audience, and situation, but also to the functions the systems provide. Students are likely to discover in their research, as we discovered in ours, that the task environments of the new systems compel writers to ask specific planning questions: Does this assignment require drafting and revising? Can I use a first-time-final strategy? Do I know an appropriate pattern to follow? Can I amend a stored form for this communication? Shall I simply record notes now and write my document later? Students should practice choosing and using a variety of planning strategies.

Encouraging different planning strategies for different kinds of assignments. Although some teachers help students learn the art of invention by teaching heuristic strategies—derived from classical rhetoric, Kenneth Burke's pentad, D. Gordon Rohman's pre-writing method, Kenneth Pike's tagmemics, or Richard Larson's inventive questions[7]—and others use textbooks which carry the writer from invention through the entire writing process—such as Corbett's *Classical Rhetoric for the Modern Student*; Flower's *Problem-Solving Strategies for Writing*; and Janice Lauer, Gene Montague, Andrea Lunsford, and Janet Emig's *Four Worlds of Writing*[8]—teachers should also emphasize the *choices* involved in picking the appropriate strategy for a specific assignment. Since writers who use the new systems have to choose the appropriate composing option, teachers should provide ongoing opportunities for students to make such choices and to discuss how they made them—in relation to purpose, audience, importance of the communication, remembered patterns of presentation, or reference to stored forms.

More specifically, teachers can introduce not only high-level invention heuristics, which are useful for planning complex written products, but also fairly standard or even stereotypic patterns suitable to routine communications and forms, for which students plan content within the constraints of an imposed style. Students should understand the different strategies involved in, for example, outlining, writing, and revising a report at home; making notes, writing, and editing an essay exam in class; and filling out a job application form in an office. And they should have as many opportunities as possible to plan different kinds of communications which require different planning strategies. In general, to prepare students to plan effectively for composing on the new systems, teachers should introduce the options afforded by the systems, showing how considerations of audience and strategies for planning are affected by the new media.

Translating Plans into Writing

Translating plans directly into writing places continual demands on long-term memory, short-term memory, and conscious attention. These demands are compounded in composing on the new systems, as our discussion of ad hoc planning in dictation has shown, when such systems depend on the oral production of written texts. Translating plans into oral statements which will become written prose forces writers to visualize the form of the printed text even while they are producing two threads of oral discourse. Writers who use such systems therefore require a tutored sensitivity to the form of written prose; they also need serviceable oral delivery skills.

Developing sensitivity to visual, syntactic, and mechanical con-

ventions of writing through reading. Dictators have to be able to retrieve from their long-term memory visual pictures of written texts—pictures which include format, syntactic, and mechanical details—and they have to be able to describe these features to a transcriptionist. Similarly, those who use electronic mail systems have to be able to emphasize—through format signals, parallel structures, and punctuation—the key points readers will see on-screen. One way students can become more proficient at visualizing written texts and using textual features effectively is by reading; as Ong says, students should "read, read, read. There is no way to write unless you read, and read a lot."[9]

Reading, reading aloud, narrating what was read, and describing the features of a printed text: These are activities teachers should encourage. While Britton asserts that writers naturally develop "an inner voice capable of dictating . . . the forms of written language,"[10] teachers can help students cultivate an "inner eye" as well by drawing their attention to formal conventions of printed text: spelling, mechanics, headings, white space, numbered lists, underscores. (Oral composers need an especially strong sense of format to visualize their messages and to translate their visualizations into directions for the transcriptionist.) In any reading they do—a story, a play, a newspaper article, a procedures manual, a letter—students should be encouraged to notice and internalize conventions of written texts so that they can visualize and use them as the occasion demands. Although we are certainly not proposing that reading be substituted for writing as the primary activity in composition classes, we do endorse the use of student and professional models as described by Eschholz, who concludes: "Models can be a positive and useful device in teaching students to write better if they are thoughtfully and purposefully integrated into the individual student's writing process."[11]

To help students develop a flexible range of syntactic structures, teachers can encourage sensitivity to style, register, and differences between dialogic and monologic discourse by emphasizing these features in written texts. As Moffett has pointed out, a classroom rich in language experience allows students to make connections between the literature they have read and the writing and speaking they will do.[12] But more specifically, when teachers help students recognize differences between intimate and formal patterns of discourse or between context-dependent and context-independent verbal statements, they are also laying the groundwork for effective written and oral performance.[13]

Furthermore, students should demonstrate evidence of their reading in the papers they write. They should use appropriate, accurate spelling and mechanics to enable a reader to move easily through a text. By attending to visual, syntactic, and mechanical conventions while reading, students are likely to improve their written work, whether it originates as writing or speaking.

Developing oral skills. Throughout this discussion, we have emphasized speaking as an important component of composing and have offered suggestions for incorporating speaking in composition courses. Although various authors have shown that speaking can help students explore their ideas, clarify and expand the meaning of their writing, and improve their written texts,[14] and although we would encourage any activity that improves writing, we are specifically interested in helping students learn oral delivery skills they will use on the new communication systems.

Composition teachers can offer their students many opportunities to develop oral skills. For example, students can learn to take notes in small group discussions and use these notes when reporting group observations to the class. Or they can develop short presentations, enhanced with graphic aids, to summarize their research findings for other students. Or they can analyze ineffective writing and compose revisions orally. Or they can read their essays aloud, using their voices to punctuate their messages. Oral presentations, whether formal or informal, develop highly transferable skills—memory skills, delivery skills, and listening skills—which are useful in any communicative situation and essential in composing on the new dictation, audio mail, and teleconferencing systems.

The translation skills required by the new systems may seem quite different from those usually emphasized in freshman composition classes. However, visualization and oral delivery are based on reading, observing, and writing, the basic content of English courses. The challenge for teachers is to extend that content by cultivating skills which students can readily transfer to other contexts.

Reviewing

To compose effective writing on the new systems, students need experience with a wide range of reviewing strategies which they can apply as needed—when revising a tape, editing on a word processor, or correcting a printout. They also need experience in collaborating with others—in planning, in translating, and especially in reviewing their writing.

Developing a variety of auditory and visual reviewing strategies. Our research shows that writers who use the new communication systems to compose written texts review their work on tapes, at word processing video screens, and in drafts; they review to relisten or reread—for direction, content, style, and tone—so that they can move forward, just as we are doing as we write this chapter; they also review to revise, edit, and correct.

For effective auditory reviews, writers need listening skills which will allow them to focus on meaning and style. To help students concentrate on the meaning of a spoken text, E. D. Hirsch recommends reading printed prose aloud in composition classes. Since "the listener is unable to circle back and reprocess an earlier section,"[15] he learns to concentrate on the message as it unfolds, noting difficult or incomprehensible passages. Similarly, James Collins shows that close listening—by students *and* teachers—will lead to classes and conferences which illuminate the meaning of written drafts.[16] And Elbow recommends listening to drafts to isolate strong and weak passages and to improve style.[17] Our own experience in teaching freshman composition suggests that cultivating listening skills can also encourage creativity and sensitivity to language.[18] Developing listening skills, then, will prepare students not only for the systems they will use after college but also for learning and writing in college.

Visual review has been studied much more thoroughly than auditory review, mainly within the context of revision as a recursive process of insight and reformulation. Our research suggests that, because writers who use the new systems typically plan their texts in advance, revision of this kind is usually limited to drafting long or complex texts. Writers who compose shorter communications at electronic mail terminals revise and edit very little;[19] writers who orally compose shorter, less complex writing tend to edit locally on tape and check for content or mechanical errors on printed copy. Therefore, in addition to teaching students large-scale revision strategies, teachers should also emphasize visual and auditory strategies for editing and correcting.

Since our research shows that reviewers tend to revise content while overlooking style, teachers would be wise to emphasize stylistic evaluation as an intrinsic part of the reviewing process. Teachers can help students become familiar with various styles of discourse by encouraging reading and intelligent discussion, and especially by emphasizing the stylistic options that writers exercise. Sentence combining is one technique likely to prove useful in highlighting options for developing a specific sentence within a specific context.[20] Certainly, attention to cohesion features and to the effects of style on readers will emphasize the importance of stylistic consideration in reviewing.[21] In any case, consistent attention to style is likely to help students focus their auditory and visual reviews on this frequently neglected aspect of revision.

In this connection, teachers whose students have access to computer terminals can include text-editing programs to emphasize important stylistic matters. The Writer's Workbench programs, developed by Bell Laboratories, help writers attend to sentence structure, awkward or wordy phrases, repetitious vocabulary, and spelling; according to William Weiss, Writer's Workbench "raises standards for writing by giving writers more incentive to polish" their work.[22] Text-editing programs at UCLA, Notre Dame, and elsewhere have also helped student writers improve their reviewing strategies by concentrating on style.[23]

Whatever methods teachers choose, developing auditory and visual review strategies is likely to help students produce polished writing, in composition classes, in other classes, and in their post-college writing.

Providing constant opportunities for collaboration. Writers who use the new systems collaborate often with others and interact with a variety of media throughout the composing process. Sometimes composing requires solitude—an individual with pen poised over a blank page. But more often composing occurs in busy places: crowded newsrooms with dozens of reporters typing at word processing terminals; doctors' offices with phones ringing and tape recorders switched on between patient visits; teleconferencing centers with scores of people watching television screens, talking on phone hookups, and writing notes on scratch pads. Since on-the-job writing often occurs in active, highly collaborative settings, students can benefit from the experience of working with others and with a variety of media.

We have suggested above several possibilities for collaboration with other students. When discussing planning, we recommended group work and media activities. In translating, we mentioned reading to others and making group presentations. For reviewing, revising, and editing, we recommend peer evaluation strategies.[24] Koch and Brazil offer suggestions for incorporating collaborative activities throughout the composing process.[25] But we would also encourage teachers to provide opportunities for collaboration with media. Many teachers, of course, use tape recorders, transparencies, film strips, video tapes, and other media in their teaching. They should also offer students opportunities to use these media when making presentations. If tape recorders and word processing terminals are available, teachers should encourage students to use them while composing.

Teachers can also consider using media to improve the writing of individual students. Our research suggests, for example, that students who have difficulty revising their writing might benefit from composing on tape recorders with audible fast-forward features and reviewing their work, especially for meaning and coherence, before transcribing it. Such a practice would enable students who tend toward nonlinear patterns of conceptualization to review quickly, before losing the thread of their thinking, to reconsider an entire text before writing or typing it, and to consider improvements as they transcribe. The medium thereby organizes reviewing and revision for the student. Our research also suggests that certain text-editing programs may help students focus more deliberately on style and spelling. For example, certain revision-stage programs call attention to the repetition of words or sentence patterns. And dictionary programs such as The WORD Plus help poor spellers identify patterns of error and improve their spelling.[26] Used in these ways, the media we have been discussing will not only introduce students to systems they will use in the future but may also enhance their learning in composition classes.

To summarize our discussion of reviewing, then, we would emphasize three points: that students should learn a variety of reviewing, revising, and editing strategies; should work collaboratively sometimes to simulate the environment of the workplace; and should experiment with various media to improve their speaking and writing.

The teaching goals we have discussed in this section are intended to introduce students to the kinds of composing they are likely to do in the future. We have attempted to show how teachers, within the context of a freshman composition course, can make connections between reading, writing, speaking, and listening that will engage students in learning and, at the same time, develop transferable composing skills.

We would now like to demonstrate how these goals can be incorporated in a performance objective. Our purpose here is two-fold: to present a specific assignment which incorporates the goals we have discussed, and to offer teachers a way to estimate whether they have achieved their goals as measured by student performance.

Designing and Using a Specific Performance Objective

Translating teaching goals into performance objectives is like translating writing plans into written sentences. It is a goal-directed process bounded by several constraints. In place of the syntactic and contextual constraints associated with forming acceptable English sentences, performance objectives are limited by operational constraints intended to establish a correspondence between teaching goals and student performance. According to Richard Young, a performance objective which translates goals into actions should: (1) name the performance desired; (2) describe any significant constraints on the performance; (3) specify the level of performance; and (4) be understandable to the students without additional explanation.[27] Working within these constraints, teachers should be able to formulate performance objectives which reflect the goals established above. To evaluate our success in reaching the teaching goals for students in a freshman composition class, we constructed the following performance objective:

> After reading about new communication systems and investigating differences between speaking and writing, students will be able to write guidelines for users of audio mail, a system which records oral messages for an absent audience.

To convert this performance objective into a class assignment, we combined a variety of activities: reading, class discussions, speaking and writing exercises, and peer group evaluations.

As an introduction to the communication systems they will encounter on their jobs, students read an informative article by Mertes, "Doing Your Office Over—Electronically," from the *Harvard Business Review*.[28] The article shows how a large Chicago bank introduced dictation/word processing systems, electronic mail, data bases, and audio mail to improve its overall operation. After discussing this article, students concluded that while the new technology may speed the communication process, the effectiveness of the communicated product depends on the spoken and written skills of the users. To develop speaking and writing skills while learning more about one new communication system, audio mail, students spent three 50-minute class periods working through each of two hypothetical situations that we developed, one for speaking and one for writing. In each, we deliberately varied the context, audience, and purpose.

For the context of the *speaking assignment*, students assumed the role of branch manager of a nationwide student credit union, SCU, whose graphic design department was sponsoring a logo contest. Students were to create designs for a new logo according to certain specifications and to prepare to describe their designs to a graphic artist by leaving a message on the company's audio mail system.[29] The purpose of the message was to describe the design orally so that the graphic artist could reproduce it and enter it in the contest. We encouraged students to sketch their designs and to outline or think through their messages for the artist but asked them not to write out instructions in longhand. (See appendix H for a copy of the assignment, Using Audio Mail.)

The next day, students reported to our offices, two at a time, to record their designs on tape recorders, simulating audio mail. After recording their messages, students traded tapes, listened to each other's description, and tried to reproduce the logo. Students evaluated the quality of instructions for the design as well as the message as a whole. They then compared their drawings with the original sketches.

During the next class period, students discussed their experience with audio mail on several levels. First, they identified characteristics of good directions, including precise language (in the upper left-hand corner of the square, a quarter of an inch away from the sides) and use of similes (entwined like the symbol for the Olympics). Second, they discussed important information, in addition to the design directions, that the receiver of the audio message would need, such as identification of the caller, the purpose of the call, the desired action, and the deadline. Several students had omitted such information from their tapes, despite instructions to leave a *complete* message. Finally, students compared speaking and writing by discussing whether audio mail was more like a phone call or more like a letter. They concluded that audio mail is a unique mixture of both. Like speaking, audio mail is oral, quick-paced, and offers little chance for deliberation or revision. Like writing, audio mail addresses an absent audience, requires an autonomous message, and can be planned in advance. That the speaking assignment for audio mail increased the students' awareness of the different skills involved in speaking and writing is reflected in this student's observation: "Giving the audio-mail message showed me that I ignored differences [between speaking and writing] and tried to give the message as if I were having a conversation. The activity helped emphasize the differences."

For a *writing assignment* to show their understanding of the skills required for the new communication system, students wrote "Guidelines for Users of Audio Mail." (See appendix I for a copy of the writing assignment, Audio Mail: A User's Guide.) For the context and audience of the assignment, students assumed the role of a technical writer responsible for preparing training guides for employees at the credit union. The purposes of the audio mail guide were three: to describe the system, to explain the process, and to encourage callers not to hang up at the announcement of a recorded message but instead to compose a message that would accomplish the original purpose of the call. To prepare to write the user's guides, students studied user's manuals developed for on-the-job training for dictation/word processing systems. Students noted in particular the organization of the user's manuals. They discussed how the strategies they had previously studied in essays that described processes might be applied to writing a user's guide. Students also commented on how obvious format features, such as numbered lists and starred directions, as well as more subtle features, such as effective use of white space, parallel structure, and punctuation, improved readability. Finally, students discussed identifying, limiting, and arranging the content of the user's guides that they would write as a homework assignment.

During the third class period, students evaluated each other's guides in peer groups, paying particular attention to audience adaptation, completeness, and format. They were surprised to see how the same assignment describing the same process could be organized, written, and formatted in so many different ways. Finally, students revised their written guides and submitted them for our evaluation.

Evaluating the Unit Impressionistically

Not only did these two assignments help us meet our performance objective, but they also allowed us to see that we had achieved our specific teaching goals for this unit in freshman composition: to introduce students to the new systems; to provide opportunities for addressing different audiences in speaking and writing; to teach alternative planning and reviewing strategies; to develop a sensitivity to conventions of writing and format; and to encourage collaborative work. Furthermore, by asking students to complete a subjective response form, we found that they were enthusiastic about studying audio mail and enjoyed the variety this short assignment added to a course that otherwise focused on reading and writing essays. (For a tabulation of students' responses to the unit on audio mail, see appendix J.) As a matter of fact, the students' main suggestion for improving the unit was to include more instruction on other communication systems, especially electronic mail. That students will use what they learned about audio mail is certain. One student told us: "I found taping the message very useful because that same day I applied what I'd learned when I made a long distance call that was answered by a recording."

In developing this short unit for freshman composition and in emphasizing throughout the semester certain composing activities associated with the new communication media, we were guided by the general objective and the specific teaching goals outlined at the beginning of this chapter. We did not change the overall orientation of our classes, nor did we omit any of the rhetorical or composing features we typically include. But we did broaden our frame of reference and stress certain activities, such as oral presentations and collaborative work, to cultivate a wider range of verbal skills. And we did, like our students, learn a great deal from this introduction to the new technology.

Defining Teaching Goals to Introduce the New Systems in Advanced Composition Classes

In addition to developing transferable writing skills, students in professionally oriented advanced composition courses should learn the specific requirements of the new communication systems, especially as they apply to the composing process. While some teachers might argue that such career-specific training belongs in on-the-job seminars rather than college composition classes, the quality of this student's memo suggests otherwise:

> *Applicant 1* Applicant 1, shows no work experiences of any type. He was a high school drop out, and has only held a job for as long as three months at a time. He admitted he hated manual labor and admitted to not liking to be around people. His attendance record while at work was good, but I find it hard to believe he would have a good excuse for missing work when you only worked there for three months anyway. He expresses to continue his education, but is just holding out to find out if he can get a job or not. The more I learned from Applicant 1, in the interview, I feel our company has no use for him on the training program.

There is little evidence in this dictated passage that its author, a college junior, had received an "A" in freshman composition and was a "B+" student in advanced composition.[30] Research, in fact, suggests only a low correlation between the final grades students receive in advanced composition and the scores the same students receive when they dictate communications.[31] The same research shows, however, that students who receive a short unit of nontechnical instruction in adapting the composing processes they use in pen-in-hand writing to the new systems write significantly better communications than students who do not receive such instruction. Since students who have grown up in an age of television, tape recorders, computers, and video games are often eager to learn to use the new communication media, teachers of professionally oriented advanced composition courses might well consider including a short unit on such systems.

In this section, we will present a plan for teaching students to adapt the composing process they use when writing to the distinctive requirements of dictating for word processing systems. We will discuss six specific teaching goals appropriate to professionally oriented advanced composition classes:

- introducing students to dictation/word processing systems, especially to their distinctive features;
- preparing students to use a variety of advance planning strategies for dictation;
- preparing students for ad hoc planning;
- developing technical and oral skills for using dictation equipment;
- introducing auditory and visual reviewing strategies which are appropriate to different dictation options;
- encouraging collaboration with equipment and people for efficient use of dictation/word processing systems.

We will discuss these goals within the task environment of on-the-job composing and within the context of planning, translating, and revising orally produced written communications.

Task Environment

Some students in advanced courses may have worked in internships or on summer jobs where dictating for word processing systems was standard procedure; others may have parents who dictate communications on their jobs and use portable recorders at home; most will have read about such systems or seen them advertised in magazines or on television. Teachers may therefore want to call upon students to help introduce the new systems. For their own preparation, teachers will find it helpful to look through books, such as *Word Processing: A Systems Approach to the Office*,[32] and to visit a local dictation/word processing center or a nearby equipment distributor. Because word processing systems vary, students need only an overview of the general structure of such systems at this point.

Introducing students to dictation/word processing systems, especially to their distinctive features. Teachers will have to provide a detailed introduction to the dictation options available on dictation/word processing systems. Although students may have relied on a first-time-final approach to writing at 11:30 P.M. with a paper due early the next morning, they will have to learn that many factors influence composing strategies in dictation. Numerous considerations within the organizational environment affect users of the new systems: company policy, the capabilities of a particular dictation/word processing system, and cost/time constraints. So do assignment-specific considerations such as purpose, audience, complexity, and importance of the message to the writer and the organization. Students will therefore have to know that the new systems require decisions about drafting, composing first-time-final copy, adapting form communications, and recording information. Teachers should, by all means, discuss with students how these options influence the composing process of dictation.

Planning

As Vygotsky notes, "The speed of oral composing is unfavorable to a complicated process of formulation—it does not leave time for deliberation and choice."[33] By learning strategies for planning dictated communications, however, students can relieve some of the pressures of oral composing by deliberating and choosing before they speak.

Preparing students to use a variety of planning strategies for dictation. Although dictation equipment has pause and erase capabilities, such features do not replace planning, a fact documented in a survey of experienced dictators who unanimously agreed: "Your dictation can never be better than your preparation."[34] Planning for dictation includes a variety of activities: analyzing audience, determining purpose, generating ideas and gathering information, selecting and organizing materials, and attending to format and transcription signals. While these strategies are similar to those taught in writing, instructors will want to emphasize special considerations when teaching dictation.

Analyzing audience requires that students distinguish between the needs of short-term and long-term audiences. Experienced dictator George Heighway described his process for analyzing audience this way: "Before I begin to dictate . . . , I figure out what I am trying to say, who I'm trying to say it to, and what knowledge they have that I can key into."[35] Intensive training in audience analysis, following a sequence proposed by Mathes and Stevenson for technical writing and by Halpern for business writing, can help the student plan reader-based messages.[36] Furthermore, students have to develop uncommon sensitivities to style, especially as it pertains to register and speaking/writing differences when they adapt their language to different audiences.

As noted in chapter 2, the dictator conducts two concurrent monologues. To demonstrate this, an instructor can play tapes of dictated communications borrowed from associates in business, industry, or academe. After listening to the tapes, students can identify special directions given to the transcriptionist—format, capitalization, punctuation, unusual spelling. They can discuss how the dictator's shifts in spoken style distinguish instructions for the transcriptionist from the message itself; they can plan how to distinguish their oral directions from their dictated writing. Students can practice adapting their speech for dual audiences by working in groups of three: One student can read aloud a previously written communication, casually addressing a second student, the "transcriptionist," when giving typing directions for format, punctuation, or spelling, and more formally addressing the third student, the "intended reader," when speaking the written message. In general, the most effective way to convey the notion of dual audiences is through example, discussion, and practice.

Determining the purpose of a communication is not an isolated task. The dictator, like the writer, must consider topic, audience, and environmental cues. The task is further complicated since, as Knoblauch points out, most communications have "multiple purposes, the interaction of which motivates and shapes performance."[37] To help students clarify the purpose of a communication so that they can plan appropriately, teachers can introduce a series of questions:

- What is the context or issue of concern?

- Will the communication respond to previous correspondence or assignments on the issue? If so, specifically what will I have to do?

- What do I wish to accomplish with this communication?[38]

Determining purpose in this way will help students choose an appropriate dictation option and decide whether they need more elaborate invention strategies, whether a routine pattern will suffice, or whether a form will do.

Generating ideas and gathering information depend on purpose and dictation option. Drafts of complex reports or difficult first-time-final communications may require elaborate heuristics—sets of questions, tagmemics, classical invention strategies—to probe long-term memory and to arrive at new insights and creative ideas. But simple responses may require little more than filling in slots with new information.

Similarly, gathering information depends on purpose and dictation option. For complex communications, dictators report collecting files, calendars, past correspondence, notes, and related reports before beginning to dictate; they also conduct surveys, collect data, or initiate computer searches for stored information. But for routine communications, they may dictate from the letter they are answering, from a few notes, or from a mental plan. By planning a variety of messages, students soon learn how much work to do before recording a message.

Selecting and organizing materials is an important subprocess of planning; the dictator usually thinks through an entire communication in advance. The dictation option plays a role here too. Does the communication require an original organization and choices about what to include, what to put in an appendix, and what to omit? Or will an internalized pattern from the dictator's long-term memory or a form stored in a computer memory suffice?

Whether the organizational plan is original or routine, students, like most dictators, will find it useful to work from key-word outlines or brief notes. Such planning helps the dictator and the reader since, as Meyer notes, "the presence of a visible plan for presenting content plays a crucial role in assuring the interpretability of a passage."[39] Although some students routinely make outlines before writing, instructors should teach key-word outlining to show how several ideas can be condensed into one word or a short phrase. Key-word outlines trigger memory during translating, allowing the dictator to transform single words back into original thoughts. In their work on memory and language skills, Paul Fitts and Michael Posner stress that the value of an outline depends on how much information can be symbolized in a word or phrase without losing meaning: "The limitations of human memory are too great to allow storage of much untransformed information."[40] If students develop "untransformed information" into detailed outlines, they are tempted to write their communications in longhand and read them into the recorder, defeating one important reason for dictating: to save time.

A teacher can begin instruction in key-word outlining by having students briefly outline previously written communications and practice composing orally from their outlines. Since students are familiar with the content of the communications, a key-word outline should provide enough cues to reconstruct a whole message. Once students understand key-word outlining, they can practice outlining new messages and delivering them orally.

Attending to format and transcription signals is usually part of revision in writing; in dictating, however, it must be part of planning. Dictators often begin their recordings by telling the transcriptionist whether the communication is a letter, memo, or report, a draft or final copy. They consider headings, graphics, and special formatting signals such as white space, indentions, and underscores. As one experienced dictator put it: "Just as in writing with a pencil or typewriter, you must be able to visualize the final product, see it on the page."[41] Because students want their dictated messages to look like written prose, they will have to develop the habit of planning format signals for the transcriptionist.

Betty Ricks, in her survey of critical managerial communication skills, confirms that learning the planning strategies we have described is essential to the dictation process: "It is important for managers to acquire pre-dictation skills—including content selection, ability to outline responses either written or mentally, knowledge of correct grammar and appropriate word usage."[42] Furthermore, students need enough information about the systems and how they function to make intelligent choices on these matters.

Translating

If, as Flower and Hayes suggest, "the act of writing is best described as the act of juggling a number of simultaneous constraints,"[43] then students learning dictation face an even tougher challenge as they toss several more balls in the air. For in addition to the constraints of writing, dictation requires that students juggle ad hoc planning strategies, technical equipment procedures, and oral delivery skills.

Preparing students for ad hoc planning. As Arnold, interpreting Quintilian, writes:

> Speakers must at one and the same time recall their plans for communication, preserve awareness of how far the plans have been achieved and

what remains to be done, look ahead to what is required in instants to come, and do all this while maintaining precisely the intellectual, personal, and emotional relationship with listeners which immediate and longer-ranged purposes require.[44]

This process accurately describes the ad hoc planning dictators do during translating. Using short-term memory, they expand their key-word outlines into complete ideas. Using long-term memory, they select sentence patterns that allow them to speak these ideas in a style appropriate to written prose. Students can be alerted to the frequency of ad hoc planning by listening to the halting delivery of experienced dictators who pause as often as every five or six words to plan the next phrase. And they can be prepared to formulate good sentences by careful planning and, of course, by consistent practice in reading, writing, and speaking.

Developing technical and oral skills for using dictation equipment. Although it warrants relatively little attention in composition classes, the technical part of dictation is the focus of "Dictation" sections in most business writing texts.[45] Why? Probably because the technical process of dictation is easier to teach, and, with practice, to master, than the composing process. Instructions to students on using dictation equipment, however, need not be elaborate. Ideally, students should have practice with phone systems, desk-top models, and portable units. More realistically, an instructor need only describe the basic procedures used with the first two systems and borrow portable units from an equipment vendor for students to share.[46] Students can then practice addressing the transcriber, dictating unusual format instructions, adding new information, and editing sentences previously taped. Various textbooks, equipment manuals, and in-house training materials offer guidelines, exercises, and checklists to teach these procedures as well as tips on speaking clearly. (For sources on teaching dictation, see appendix K.)

Once students become adept at using the equipment, they can practice oral delivery by dictating communications they have planned. They can transcribe their own tapes, checking articulation and pace, and they can transcribe classmates' tapes, experiencing what it is like to receive an unfamiliar message. Students can also rate each other's instructions to the transcriptionist, noting unclear directions, garbled speech, or inconsistent format, spelling, or punctuation signals.[47]

During translating, students come to realize how the composing and technical processes of dictation work in harmony. They learn that they can plan their phrases and sentences by stopping the tape to think, and that they can correct false starts by taping over them. A short practice session with dictation equipment goes a long way toward helping students adjust their composing strategies to a new medium.

Reviewing

Dictation/word processing systems increase a user's options for review. She can listen to her tape, scan a draft on a video display screen, read a typed copy herself, or have several copies distributed to solicit suggestions from colleagues.

Introducing auditory and visual reviewing strategies appropriate to different dictation options. Students should learn to use auditory and visual reviewing strategies which are appropriate to the dictation option they have chosen. Since drafted communications usually require collaborative visual review, and first-time-final and form communications often require careful auditory review, students will have to learn to work with others, indicate changes on typed drafts, and correct their tapes.

While research shows that dictators who revise consistently attend to content, it also shows that they need additional training to evaluate the style of their written prose. Because dictators rely heavily on their short-term memory to recall what they have said in the previous phrase, and because they are orally translating from brief notes, certain grammatical errors are likely to occur in dictated passages. At least four such errors are present in the student's dictated paragraph quoted at the beginning of this section.

- *Faulty sentence structure*, including incomplete parallelism: "The more I learned from Applicant 1, in the interview, I feel our company has no use for him on the training program."

- *Inaccurate pronoun reference*: "His attendance record while at work was good, but I find it hard to believe he would have a good excuse for missing work when you only worked there for three months anyway."

- *Inappropriate tense switches*: "He was a high school drop out, and has only held a job for as long as three months at a time."

- *Vocabulary-related errors*, including repetition and wordiness: "He expresses to continue his education, but is just holding out to find out if he can get a job or not."

Clearly, the style of speech differs from the style of writing, but, as this sample suggests, the untutored style of dictation may be an odd blend of both. The vocabulary-related errors above illustrate an inexperienced dictator's attempt to over-correct her speech to approximate the form of written prose. The sentence begins with elliptical formal diction, "He expresses to continue," and ends with everyday speech, "find out if he can get a job or not." Students should be prepared in advance to speak writing, but they should also be prepared to revise their spoken text into written prose, with close attention to style.

Furthermore, students should learn to practice proofreading for unintentional changes or typos the transcriptionist may have made and learn how to indicate changes clearly. On the other hand, students should also, as Kenneth Mayer and Bella Clinkscale suggest, "be taught when to accept minor imperfections . . . in light of the cost and time involved" in correcting.[48]

Encouraging collaboration with equipment and people for efficient use of dictation/word processing systems. If, as Don Payne suggests, "We frighten students with writing's permanence and aloneness," then teaching them to dictate for word processing systems should do much to dispel both fears.[49] The ease with which a tape can be erased or a paragraph moved on the word processor encourages an attitude of flexibility in composing. And the frequency of collaboration—with the transcriptionist and others—encourages a spirit of cooperation that makes writing as inviting as a friendly conversation. Students can learn to collaborate on dictated communications by helping others revise their drafts (an unfamiliar text is often easier to critique); and they can learn to tinker with their phrases and sentences on tape recorders, and with their paragraphs, format, and graphics on word processors. In general, the new systems are likely to encourage reviewing because they make it so easy.

To communicate successfully on the job, students will have to learn to write, to speak, *and* to dictate. Becoming a good dictator, like becoming a good writer or a good speaker, takes practice. But students can learn strategies for planning, translating, and revising that prevent dictation from being a trial-and-error process. And they welcome the chance to learn dictation in the nonthreatening environment of the classroom.

Using a Specific Performance Objective and Assignment

Using the following performance objective is one way to measure the success of meeting teaching goals for dictation:

> After five hours of training in the composing and technical processes of dictation, students will be able to plan and dictate a first-time-final memo suitable to send to a designated audience.

To create a realistic dictation assignment based on this performance objective, teachers can ask their students to compose a real-world communication like one we recently used in our classes. We had invited Jim McCoy, a counselor at the University Placement Center, to talk with our students about locating summer internships. McCoy wrote us a memo accepting the invitation and requesting further details about the class. We transformed his request into a dictation assignment, asking students to assume our roles and dictate memos responding to McCoy's. (For a copy of McCoy's memo, see appendix L.)

The students elected to plan their memos collaboratively and to aim for first-time-final copy. When planning their memos, students completed the "Guide to Planning Effective Dictation," a worksheet designed to help them produce first-time-final copy. (For a copy of the "Guide," see appendix M.) When analyzing audience, students made certain decisions that pen-in-hand writers might attend to much later in the composing process. For example, they noted from the beginning that their communication would be a short memo, typed on English Department letterhead, using full block format—details important to the transcriptionist setting up the memo. After identifying several possible long-term audiences, the students chose to send only the original and one copy, the original to McCoy and the copy to the director of business writing. They also noted other details to tell the transcriptionist as they dictated.

Students easily determined the purpose of their memos by re-reading McCoy's communication—give McCoy the information he requested. But generating ideas and gathering information called for invention and creative problem-solving. The students decided to conduct an oral survey in class to gather the information McCoy had requested: students' classification by school, semester, and major; number of students who had worked at jobs related to their majors; and areas of interest such as business, industry, government, or the arts. They also set a date, time, and place for the presentation. Next, students brainstormed other information that McCoy might find useful, such as the fact that they had already written resumes and job application letters. By collecting such details, students were able to plan a reader-based memo, an important consideration in first-time-final messages.[50]

Working with the information they had generated, students then made a key-word outline to reflect the order and content of the memo and decided to include a chart for giving specific class information (more instructions for the transcriptionist). Finally, the students agreed that an informal, friendly style matching that of McCoy's memo would be appropriate for their dictated memo.

Following their collaborative planning, each student dictated a memo that was then transcribed by a professional typist.[51] Students met in small groups during the next class period to compare memos. Even though they had all used the same key-word outline, their memos differed in several ways: sentence structure, vocabulary, and format for the chart. Students evaluated their memos in terms of acceptable first-time-final copy: Was the content accurate and complete? Was the style appropriate for written prose? Did the format enhance readability? They also discussed how they would revise or edit their memos if given a chance. Finally, the class selected one memo to send to McCoy and awaited the results. Would McCoy come to class, on the set day, at the appointed time, with a clear understanding of the audience he was to address? He did. And furthermore, he congratulated the class on the memo. We had met our performance objective.

Conducting Research on the Effectiveness of Pedagogy

Just as our profession needs sound research to learn how writers adapt the pen-in-hand composing process to the new systems, it also needs research to evaluate how effectively students are learning the processes we are teaching. One way to gather such information is informally, as we did in our subjective evaluation of the audio mail unit in our freshman composition classes. While such evaluations can provide impressionistic assessments of teacher and student attitudes about what was learned, they do not actually measure the effectiveness of pedagogical practice in relation to teaching goals. Experimental research offers a more rigorous, objective method for evaluating pedagogical effectiveness.

In their introduction to *Research on Composing: Points of Departure*, Charles Cooper and Lee Odell point out the fallacy of conducting experimental research in the classroom to discover the best methods for teaching composition, when we know so little about the composing process itself.[52] While their argument is persuasive and may, in fact, have motivated much of the recent research on composing, classroom research remains a useful way to test our theories and models and to increase our knowledge of how writers learn to write.

To see if the teaching goals and pedagogical practices detailed in our unit for advanced composition classes actually helped students learn to dictate, we conducted an experiment in our business writing classes at Purdue University. Our purpose in conducting the classroom experiment was not to discover if teaching dictation one way is better than another. Rather, we wanted to see if what we had learned in our descriptive research on dictation could be applied to teaching. Our hypothesis was that students taught both the composing and technical processes of dictation would produce significantly better communications than students taught only the technical process. While this hypothesis may at first seem self-evident, it is based on two assumptions: (1) Dictation requires adaptations in the composing process of writing, especially in planning; and (2) Students can learn to make these adaptations. We tested our hypothesis in the following way.

Design, Subjects, and Treatments

Four classes of business writing students, two classes per time period, took part in the experiment. The students were a heterogeneous group: males and females; sophomores, juniors, and seniors; students from a variety of schools in the university including Agriculture; Consumer and Family Science; Humanities, Social Science, and Education; Management; Supervision; and Technology. We randomly assigned the 84 students to either a treatment or a control group. Each of us taught two classes, one treatment and one control.

We conducted the experiment after students had received two months of instruction on *writing* memos and reports. In four class hours, we taught the treatment group strategies for planning, translating, and reviewing dictated communications, with an emphasis on planning. We used handouts, transparencies, assignments, and tapes of dictated communications to teach the composing process of dictation. Although we sometimes encouraged students in the treatment group to compose aloud, they never dictated complete, original communications and had no advantage of practice over the control group. During the same time period, we reviewed with the control group the rhetorical context of the composing process, emphasizing writer, message, and audience. We used handouts, assignments, and taped communications in the lessons. Essentially, the control group reviewed principles of writing similar to those the treatment group learned for the composing process of dictation, using the same kinds of instructional materials.

The treatment and control groups for each time period met together for one hour to learn the technical aspects of dictation. The joint sessions assured that all groups received the same training in using the dictation equipment; in informing the transcriptionist of format, punctuation, and spelling; and in speaking clearly. A Lanier sales representative furnished the portable dictation equipment and conducted the training sessions to simulate dictation instruction that on-the-job writers typically receive. After his instruction, all students practiced using the equipment and addressing the transcriptionist.

After learning the technical process of dictation, all students received the same structured assignment. They assumed the role of a job recruiter who had received a memo from the personnel director of a manufacturing company; the memo contained instructions to interview job applicants. To simulate the interviewing process, students viewed a 15-minute film in which three men applied for jobs. Students then decided which applicant(s), if any, to hire, based on their notes from the film and on information in the personnel director's memo describing the job openings and company guidelines for hiring. (See appendix N for a copy of the personnel director's memo.) The next day, the students dictated their first-time-final memos.[53] Seated alone in office cubicles and using the same dictation equipment on which they had practiced in class, students dictated their memos from outlines or notes but not from texts written beforehand. A professional transcriptionist then typed the memos.

Evaluation Methods and Results

To evaluate the quality of students' dictated memos, we trained two raters to score the memos holistically and analytically. Raters used holistic, general impression scoring to evaluate the overall effectiveness of the memos. Using a scale of one to four and a rubric with sample memos that defined each score, the two raters independently evaluated each memo. Raters then used analytic scoring to evaluate certain features of the memos which the treatment group had learned to plan as part of their training in the composing process of dictation: heading, purpose statement, summary of recommendations, body, format, grammar and mechanics, and style. Using a range of good, average, and poor, and a rubric with sample memos that defined each category, the raters independently scored the memos on each of the seven features.

To calculate results from the evaluation, we used statistical tests to analyze the holistic and analytic scores. In general, these tests showed that memos dictated by the treatment group were significantly better than those dictated by the control group. Our major hypothesis of the experiment—that students in the treatment group, taught both the composing and technical processes of dictation, would dictate better memos than students in the control group, taught only the technical process—was supported by an analysis of variance test of the holistic scores. This test showed a difference in the memo scores of the two groups at the .01 level of significance as reported on the next page in Table 3.1, Test for Differences Between Groups, Holistic Scores.

Our minor hypothesis—that specific features of the memos dictated by the two groups would differ—was supported by statistical t-tests of the analytic scores for three of the seven features: heading, purpose statement, and format. These results are reported in Table 3.2, Test for Differences Between Groups, Analytic Features. Other statistical tests showed that total analytic scores also differed at a .01

Table 3.1
Test for Differences Between Groups, Holistic Scores

Group	X̄	SD	F
Treatment	2.24	.74	9.86*
Control	2.03	.81	

Holistic scores ranged from 1 to 4.
Note:
*A difference at the .01 level of significance

Table 3.2
Test for Differences Between Groups, Analytic Features

Analytic Feature	X̄ TRTMNT	X̄ CNTRL	SD TRTMNT	SD CNTRL	t
Heading	4.98	4.46	1.04	1.29	1.99†
Purpose Statement	4.34	3.61	1.39	1.58	2.23†
Summary	5.07	4.61	1.56	1.61	1.33
Body	4.32	3.93	1.42	1.15	1.37
Format	5.41	4.59	.95	1.40	3.15*
Grammar/Mechanics	4.05	3.78	1.09	1.13	1.09
Style	4.17	3.80	1.02	1.25	1.45

Note:
*A difference at the .01 level of significance.
†A difference at the .05 level of significance.
Analytic scores for each feature ranged from 2 to 6.

level of significance. In addition, results suggest that differences between groups were not a factor of instructor variables.

To check the reliability of our evaluation methods, we calculated agreement between the raters' scores. The holistic scores had an interrater reliability correlation coefficient of r = .90 and for overall analytic scoring, r = .91.[54] According to Paul Diederich, an interrater reliability coefficient of r = .80 is high enough for program evaluation in composition.[55] Therefore, the reliability of the scoring methods is strong enough to support conclusions from the results.

Discussion

Prior to the experiment, all students had been randomly assigned to a treatment or a control group and had received the same amount and kind of training in business writing. During the experiment, all students received the same training in using the equipment, speaking clearly, and addressing the transcriptionist. Therefore, we conclude that the difference between the memo scores of the treatment group and the control group supports the importance of teaching students how to adapt the composing process of writing, particularly planning, to dictation. The treatment group's ability to dictate memos with more effective headings, purpose statements, and formats further demonstrates the importance of teaching planning strategies for dictation. A correct heading indicates that the dictator identified the primary and secondary audiences by name and role, the date, and the topic and purpose of the memo as reflected in the subject line. An effective purpose statement shows that the dictator analyzed the context, task, and purpose for writing the memo. A well-formatted memo suggests that the dictator signaled paragraphs, spacing, underlining, and/or special features such as starred lists or charts. Superior performance on these three features by students in the treatment group reflects careful planning.[56]

Our conclusion that students benefited from studying the composing process of dictation is further supported by students' written evaluations. In a questionnaire completed immediately after the experiment, a majority of the students in both groups agreed with the statement: "I had no trouble using the dictation equipment." However, only in the treatment group did a majority of students agree with the statement: "I planned my dictation well." Our results showed that teaching students to adapt the pen-in-hand process to composing on the new systems improved their performance.

In discussing freshman and professionally oriented advanced composition, we have attempted to describe how teachers can use research on the new communication systems to formulate teaching goals. We have also shown how such goals can be translated into performance objectives and assignments. Finally, we have demonstrated how experimental research can allow teachers to test the effectiveness of their methods.

We have, however, purposely avoided notions of a futuristic classroom where assignments are sent by electronic mail and where each student has a computer with word processing and printout capabilities. We have also tried to avoid making composition teachers feel that they are too far behind the times to catch up with the rapidly changing technology. Unlike Northrop Frye who writes, "When I read symposia by technical experts telling me what the world will be like 100 years from now, I feel . . . as though I were in Noah's flood climbing a tree,"[57] we, as teachers of composition, have a sturdy ark in the cognitive process model of composing, a model that can accommodate the changes brought about by new technological systems. As teachers of composition, we still have the same subject to teach—writing. But we also have a responsibility to conduct research that will allow us to teach writing as it will be used by our students now—and in the future.

4

The New Technologies Offer Challenging Prospects for Research

MANY ELECTRONIC SYSTEMS AWAIT OUR RESEARCH: WORD PROcessors, electronic mail, information retrieval systems, teletext cable connections, teleconferencing networks. Technical words, these, and perhaps too futuristic to attract the interest of many teachers in our profession. But they are no more technical than "television" or "computers" or "communication satellites" or "space shuttles" were a generation ago. Nor are they as futuristic as many teachers think.

On 28 January 1982, we participated in a day-long international teleconference for on-the-job writers which discussed each of the systems mentioned above, and more.[1] The teleconference included 1,230 participants in 22 large cities in Canada and the United States. Speakers described the new technologies from the main conference site in Dallas, and the rest of us—in Toronto, Boston, Philadelphia, Atlanta, Chicago, San Francisco, Los Angeles, Vancouver—asked questions over the telephone and received immediate on-screen answers. Isaac Asimov, author of over 200 books on science, including several dozen science fiction novels, opened the discussion with a talk entitled, "Of Time, Space, and Other Things." In his talk, Asimov emphasized this theme: "Electronic communication is the greatest, most far-reaching transformation thus far in history . . . with the potential of further humanizing the global community by putting each individual in contact with the rest of the world."

From our conference site in Indianapolis, we asked the speakers this question: "Are there certain communication skills that students should learn in college which will help them adapt to this transformation in communications?" Answers by the panelists included the following points: "Thinking is the main skill students will need—to gather, organize, and disseminate information"; "Students will need creativity to synthesize, plan, and present their messages effectively"; "The next generation will embrace the technology easily—watch them now, as they play the most complicated video games. What they'll need to learn in college are the thinking and planning strategies that will make the technology work for them."[2]

If we are to believe those in the forefront of technological change, the challenge to our profession is clear: We will have to help our students develop cognitive processes they can adapt to the incredible technological changes they will confront in their lives—not technical skills that are system-specific, but thought processes that are versatile, flexible, and adaptable to a wide range of technologies. Our research on dictation systems suggests that the new technologies will rely heavily on reading, writing, speaking, and listening, perhaps in new combinations and with new emphases. It suggests, further, that processes such as creative problem-solving, planning, organizing, and using language effectively will be more crucial in the future than any of us can easily imagine.

The burgeoning white-collar work force will, as Toffler and others have pointed out, be immersed in processing information. For those of us responsible for teaching composition, technological change will mean that more students of varying abilities and ages will have to be taught to think, write, and speak effectively.[3] In this connection, the very technologies we have been discussing may come to our rescue as pedagogical tools, as devices for individualizing instruction in invention, style, grammar, spelling, and mechanics. But in other, perhaps more significant ways, the new technology is likely to help us as well—in suggesting new directions for productive research, in encouraging us to establish useful connections between the classroom and the world at large, and in justifying our professional pursuits.

Suggesting New Directions for Productive Research

At the end of chapter 2, we listed 11 questions that emerged from our investigation of how writers compose on the new dictation systems. These questions suggest three central considerations for research: developing interdisciplinary research projects, choosing appropriate research methods to investigate the effects of the new technologies on writing, and selecting settings, clientele, and topics for such research. We would now like to explain how teachers of writing can incorporate these considerations in their research.

Developing Interdisciplinary Projects

Understanding the effects of the new communication media depends on some understanding of the technology itself; it also requires attention to related research in business, computer science, cognitive psychology, oral communication, linguistics, and organizational behavior. Future research in composing is therefore likely to benefit from collaborative, interdisciplinary efforts. While there is some precedent for interdisciplinary research—in the work of Flower and Hayes, one from English and the other from psychology, in journals such as *Educational Psychologist* and *Educational Technology*, and in some of the newer anthologies, such as Hartley's *The Psychology of Written Communication* and Kroll and Vann's *Exploring Speaking-Writing Relationships*—we will have to extend our professional alliances with those who are conducting research in related fields. Ideally, such collaborations might bring together in joint authorship people in such fields as computer technology, psychology, and composition. And it might, as it did in our project, draw on the expertise of people in such fields in a less formal way. We consulted, for example, people at Purdue University and Louisiana State University from the departments of Computer Science on technical information, Education on research design, Mathematics on statistical analysis, Psychology on memory research, and Communications on oral delivery. Futhermore, we gathered information from people in business and government who were in charge of overseeing and reporting on the use of the new technology in their organizations. In a world where writing is so tightly intertwined with other activities and where research is so rapidly advancing on many fronts, the need for interdisciplinary cooperation stands out as an essential, perhaps the most essential, requirement for research on the effects of technological change on writing.

Choosing Research Methods

We can gain insight into the practices and needs of writers through concurrent and thorough research on several fronts—theoretical, historical, descriptive, and experimental.

New theoretical studies should explore appropriate professional responses to change, useful directions for interdisciplinary investigations, applications of classical rhetoric to writing and speaking vis-à-vis the new media, and the potential the new systems hold for humanistic education. For example, we will have to consider invention within a wider context, a context which includes a fuller range of composing options, and in which invention heuristics are flexible enough to incorporate the novel demands and the changing features of composing on the new systems.

New historical studies should demonstrate how change has affected composing in the past. We found, for example, the work of Ong, Corbett, and Gere essential to our understanding of this latest in a series of changes brought about by technology. Ong's discussion of the effects of printing on one of the staples of Renaissance reading, the commonplace book, was especially helpful in demonstrating how the technology of printing virtually transformed the logic, ordering, contents, and format of a specific genre.[4] We have, however, found little comparable research on typewriters, telephones, or television.[5] Surely, these media have influenced writing. Investigating them carefully is likely to offer insight into the effects of the newer technologies on oral and written composing.

Descriptive research should investigate the activities of those who compose in a variety of ways for a variety of reasons. Such research might include ethnographic or naturalistic studies, case studies including protocol analysis, field studies, longitudinal studies, and content analysis of messages. Case studies conducted in laboratory settings, such as those of Flower and Hayes, Gould, and Matsuhashi, can bring the composing process under close scrutiny, albeit in an artificial environment, and provide useful insights into the intricacies of cognitive activities. Descriptive field studies conducted in the workplace, such as those of Faigley and Miller, Odell and Goswami, and Van Dyke, can raise and answer important research questions. For example, Faigley and Miller, in their field study of 200 people in various occupations, examined not only *what* on-the-job writers composed but also *how* they composed, a procedure which led them to conclude: "electronic technology will have long-range effects on writing."[6]

Furthermore, some of the most enlightening descriptive studies are those conducted by people who actually participated in on-the-job writing projects, such as Knoblauch and Siegel, and drew from their own experience extremely useful insights about the collaborative nature of on-the-job writing.[7] Would it be too rash to suggest that college teachers, like their students, participate in internship programs to gain first-hand experience with composing in business, industry, and government? This enterprise would be comparable to the experience of teachers who attended the Bay Area Projects and actually wrote what they were asking their students to write; these teachers were, in a sense, in school, doing several kinds of academic writing. It is likely that experience in on-the-job settings, where college graduates will do most of their writing, would offer equally valuable rewards in descriptive research.[8]

And finally, a close examination of the products written or dictated by writers in different occupations, especially when multiple drafts are available, is likely to shed new light on how writers compose using different media. For example, the transformation of written material into simplified graphic form—a process hardly touched upon in our profession—is becoming increasingly widespread because of word processing and teleconferencing.[9] Examining a series of drafts of such communications will allow us to track this and other kinds of revisions writers now make on their jobs and provide further insight into the effects of technological change on writing.

Experimental research, including both true and quasi experiments, has not been conducted widely in our profession. However, recent experimental studies, like the one described in chapter 3, suggest that experimental research can be used to test the effectiveness of pedagogies derived from theoretical and descriptive investigations. Similarly, experiments can be designed to evaluate the effectiveness of written messages of different kinds.[10] And finally, experimental research can provide important information on the effects of the medium on the writer, reader, speaker, listener, or viewer. As Dell Hymes explains, "We really know very little as to the role of the medium of language. . . . We need particularly to know the meanings of media relative to one another within the context of given roles, settings, and purposes."[11] Drawing on descriptions of composing by those who write, dictate, and use word processors in their work,[12] researchers will be able to design useful experiments which identify differences in the effectiveness of messages produced with different media.

Theoretical, historical, descriptive, and experimental research which directly addresses the relationships between the new technologies and writing will open new trails of investigation for those daring enough to follow them.

Selecting Research Settings, Clientele, and Topics

Investigating the effects of electronic media on composing will require new combinations of research activities—in the library, in the offices of researchers in other disciplines and professions, in the lab, in the classroom, and especially on the job. In the past few years, studies of on-the-job writers have multiplied; similarly, research associated with writing across the curriculum has used as its touchstone the kinds of writing that college graduates do in specific disciplines. The two settings in which research on technological change is likely to flourish are in the workplace and in academe. While the studies referred to most frequently in this book prove that the workplace is an appropriate setting for descriptive research in composition, research in the academic setting may prove equally productive, for often the very electronic media which are changing communications in banks, hospitals, and government agencies are being used in colleges and universities for administration, research, and teaching.

In writing this book, we began our research in the personnel office at Purdue University. We took the short course in word processing, interviewed staff members about how the new electronic systems were affecting their writing, and used the personnel library, which contained collections of magazines and journals we had never read before—*Datamation, Modern Office Procedures, The Office,* and *Word Processing Systems.* Though our use of the academic workplace was largely a feel-your-way-around enterprise, others have conducted more organized studies on the applications of the new technology in administration and research.[13] A vast, unexplored territory awaits the imaginative researcher—in the professional schools, where public health administrators dictate their reports, where management faculty use data processing and word processing systems around the clock to write economic forecasts, where engineers design graphic aids and compose collaborative reports using computers, and where law faculty and students tap into elaborate storage and retrieval systems. Furthermore, universities are organizing teleconferences and interactive instructional productions which rely heavily on the new telecommunications technology—to teach farmers about the newest pesticides, to keep doctors informed on recent developments in epidemiology, and to apprise dentists of new clinical techniques. One need not leave campus to learn about or conduct useful research on new electronic media; in this field, the media have come to the researcher.

And so have the users of electronic systems. Those who use the new media—whether they be top administrators, faculty members, librarians, news service personnel, or clerical staff—offer a virtually untapped source of research information. Combining studies of these groups with studies of other on-the-job writers is likely to produce useful cumulative results on the effects of the new technology on the white-collar work force. Finally, there are, of course, our students, who have borne the brunt of our research efforts thus far and who are likely to continue as the main subjects of our descriptive and experimental studies.

Topics for research in technological change are as diverse as the new technologies themselves. In this book, we have explored the effects of a single new system on the composing process, and we have listed at the beginning of this chapter several other important systems which warrant consideration. But many intriguing questions about the effects of the new technology on writing remain. For example, what changes occur when students have access to bibliographic retrieval systems instead of card catalogues and index books for their research papers? In writing this book, we used, among other methods, computerized bibliographic searches of several data bases: ABI/INFORM, ERIC, Dissertation Abstracts, Language and Language Behavior Abstracts, and Management Contents. We thereby had at our disposal important literature we would not have thought to consider: for example, articles from the *Harvard Business Review, Harvard Educational Review, Management World,* and *Nation's Business,* as well as dissertations from business, communications, and psychology. Or what will happen when, as Peter McWilliams whimsically suggests, students have access to term paper data banks from which they can buy papers stored on tape, flavor them with a personal style at the word processor, and turn them in to unsuspecting teachers?[14] More seriously, the topics for research in our field are likely to range from new ways of incorporating oral performance in composition classes to new ways of teaching students to read efficiently enough to use the nontechnical but often complex documentation that accompanies word processing programs. And future research is likely to include close, interdisciplinary examination of long-term and short-term memory, especially as it operates in written and oral composing. Because the new technology is at a creative stage in its development, our profession has the opportunity and the responsibility to match it with equally creative research on composing.

Establishing Useful Connections Between the Classroom and the World at Large

The research pursuits we have suggested are likely to offer several benefits to the students we teach. By forcing us to look beyond the sentence, the paragraph, and the essay, such research will open a new window to the outside world. It will suggest readings and topics for student investigation which are related to the lives they are living and the lives they will live. Stories by Isaac Asimov and Arthur Clarke can be carefully selected and skillfully combined with short nonfiction readings about electronic media in speaking and writing assignments that underscore the possible consequences of technological change. Short writing assignments, like those we developed for the audio mail unit described above, can be based on subjects students know something about, yet allow them to extend their knowledge by reading and writing. Research assignments in which students conduct structured interviews and related library research, then share their findings with classmates, will enlighten the class as well as the instructor. Our aim here is not to provide a grab bag of pedagogical ideas but to suggest that when teachers look beyond the accustomed topics of composition research, they will discover new ways of engaging student interest by making connections between writing in school and writing beyond school.

Furthermore, such research is likely to change the focus of some composition classes by introducing new approaches to teaching. When, for example, we were involved several years ago in an extended oral biography project, we arranged for an instructional development grant which allowed us to use tape recorders in teaching an advanced composition course in oral biography and oral history. Students created their own research projects, conducted and recorded dozens of interviews, did research in the library, and produced finished products, some so polished that they became part of archival collections or were published. Because they had read oral histories and biographies such as Studs Terkel's *Working* and Merle Miller's *Plain Speaking*, the students felt that they were conducting research as writers actually do. Currently, we are teaching a course in advanced composition in which students are reading Tracy Kidder's *The Soul of a New Machine* and writing papers on how the new technology is affecting the professions they will be entering. Similarly, teachers who have become interested in word processing or telecommunications have been able to build successful courses around these media.[15] Others have developed televised courses for continuing education.

We have also found that when research on the new technology finds its way into the classroom, it encourages improvement and provides motivation for learning new composing strategies. For instance, Mimi Schwartz reports that using word processors to teach writing can "reduce initial fears of making mistakes, and . . . encourage a great willingness to explore meanings."[16] Furthermore, in the short dictation unit introduced in our business writing classes, students consistently agreed that the strategies they learned would be useful to them in the future.

Finally, of course, teachers who have investigated the new media are in a better position to prepare themselves and their students for the future. They can raise legitimate questions about the effects of technology on human beings and discuss these questions in class. They can identify communication options students are likely to encounter on their jobs and discuss which is most suitable in a specific situation. They can, with some authority, underscore with specific examples the need for creativity and problem-solving in on-the-job writing. And they can introduce a wider range of composing options, some relying entirely on memory, others on oral presentation, and still others on pen-in-hand composing. Teachers who have, through their own research, explored the world of writing as it now exists will be better able to make connections between the temporary world of writing in school and the long-term world of writing after school.

Justifying Professional Pursuits

Rather than suggesting that the wind of technological change is bringing a stormy season for reading, writing, listening, and speaking, our research has shown that these four communication skills will be absolutely essential in the years to come. The quintessentially dehumanizing activities associated with assembly line production are likely to be supplanted by other activities which depend in large measure on literacy, problem-solving, and imagination. Assuming that the technical skills required to use the new media will be learned routinely—at home, where people learn to use telephones and tape recorders, or on the job, where they learn to use specific kinds of teleconferencing and word processing equipment—teachers of English will be free to concentrate on their traditional professional pursuits with enough flexibility to accommodate change.

Clearly, reading will be essential. In the largest sense, it will be essential to develop insight into the impact of change on the quality of life. Only reading can prepare those who will be leaders in the future to make wise decisions, based not only on marketplace considerations but also on human well-being. One of the most interesting issues raised repeatedly in the literature on the new communication systems is concern for the human consequences of technological change.[17] How will computers affect roles and relationships in the workplace? How can the new technologies be used to encourage creativity? What are the educational applications and consequences of technological change?[18] Answering such questions requires insight which can only be cultivated by reading—of literature, history, sociology, and other humanistic disciplines.

Similarly, practical reading skills will be necessary for people to communicate well. Our own research has shown that those who use dictation equipment rely on internalized patterns of printed texts—graphic, syntactic, and stylistic—to speak messages that will look like writing. Also, those who learn to use the new technology will have to be able to read complex material with high comprehension at a reasonable speed. A student at Stanford Law School recently told us that he was amazed to discover, when composing a law review article on the computer, how important reading was, in this case reading the documentation accompanying his text-editing program! Another student at the University of Michigan described the process of translating written reports of geographic surveys into computerized graphic form.[19] The new technology is likely to require reading skills indirectly or directly related to the professions our students choose to enter, skills which cut across all professions and are essential for success.

Writing will be an equally important skill in a society based on communication. Whether in electronic or printed form, messages written in English, now the main language of international trade, will enable people throughout the world to communicate rapidly and, one hopes, effectively. In addition to teaching freshman and advanced writing classes at colleges and universities, teachers will be called upon increasingly to teach nontraditional students in nontraditional settings. They may find themselves teaching full-time workers in weekend programs, housewives in shopping centers, and on-the-job writers in the workplace, in the United States and abroad.[20]

Furthermore, teachers may find themselves incorporating in their classes not only the traditional material of college composition courses but also material on dictation, oral presentation, and listening. Although speech communication programs in many colleges offer courses in oral presentation, it is likely that speaking and writing will be so intertwined in the new media that composition teachers will have to address connections between the two modes in a direct way and provide more opportunities for students to learn from one another by speaking and listening. While our research on dictation systems demonstrates the need for consistent instruction in speaking and writing, our experience at the teleconference described above provides another example. Not only did we receive printed material to accompany the talks given by panelists at the central studio site, but we saw on the television screens printed outlines, charts, graphs, and electronic displays of printed text, and we responded by phone to the talks we heard and the graphics we saw. The new media are combining speaking and writing; in our composition classes, we will probably be doing the same in the years to come.

In introducing this book, we said that the main question now facing our profession is how to determine appropriate and productive responses to technological change. The answers we have presented are two. We can respond to change by conducting careful research which describes the world of writing as it now exists and pinpoints areas we will have to address in our teaching. And we can develop new and effective pedagogies which respond to our research findings. As we have shown in this chapter, the relationship between research and teaching is, like Möbius strip, continuous; neither ever ends.[21] If you take a pair of scissors to a Möbius strip and cut it lengthwise, you will find that on the first cut you produce a strip twice as long, and on the second cut you produce two strips of the same length which are looped together. Möbius strips, like the new communication technologies, are complicated. Mathematicians have found it useful to map the intricacies of Möbius strips one by one, to figure out why changes occur, and to identify the implications of these changes for other fields.

Similarly, those of us who teach writing would be wise to move carefully through the new communication systems, learn how and why they are likely to affect our profession, and apply what we have learned to our teaching. As Ong observes, "in the present and future as we live with the electronic media, we are finding and will find that these have not wiped out anything but simply complicated everything endlessly."[22] If we are to cut through the complications introduced by the new technologies, we will have to address them in our research, synthesize our findings, and apply what we learn to our teaching. To keep our profession alive within the context of change, we have much exciting work ahead.

Appendixes
Notes
Selected Bibliography

Appendix A
Interview List: Administrators, Systems Supervisors, and Transcriptionists*

Anderson, Robert G., President, Anderson's Paint and Decorating Company, 7 July 1980, Ann Arbor, MI.

Bates, Cheryl, Administrative Secretary, Harris, Lax and Gregg, Attorneys-at-Law, 8 July 1980, Ann Arbor, MI.

Bates, Percy, Assistant Deputy Director, United States Department of Education, 19 Aug. 1980, Washington, DC.

Botts, Lee, Chairman, GLBC, 6 July and 5 Aug. 1980.

Boyd, Linda, Secretary, Credit Department, MDSI, 1 July 1980.

Bunting, Kirk, Credit Assistant, MDSI, 1 July 1980.

Desenfantes, Gloria, Manager, Dictation and Word Processing Services, SFI, 29 Aug. 1980.

Doolin, Colleen, Supervisor, Word Processing Center, MBT, 11 July 1980, and 13 Aug. 1980.

Duncan, Jonna, Executive Assistant to Vice-President, MDSI, 1 July 1980.

Galler, Bernard A., Professor of Computer and Communication Sciences, Associate Director, University of Michigan Computing Center, and Editor-in-Chief, *Annals of the History of Computing*, 6 June and 28 July 1980, Ann Arbor, MI.

*For abbreviation key, see page 95.

94   Appendix A

Heighway, George, Director, Division of Health Facilities, ISBH, 31 July 1980.
Hurst, Robert, Division Manager, Metro West, MBT, 11 July 1980.
Jennette, Peggy, Supervisor, Word Processing Center, MDSI, 1 July 1980.
Koers, Mary, Chief, Agency Correspondence Section, ISBH, 31 July 1980.
Manes, Jack L., Jr., Vice-President, Human Resources, MDSI, 1 July 1980.
McIntire, Earl, Credit Manager, MDSI, 1 July 1980.
McKenzie, Alan, Associate Professor of English and Chairman of Word Processing Committee, Purdue University, 23 July 1980.
Meyer, Louis, Water Resources Planner, GLBC, 26 June 1980.
Monteith, Tim, Water Resources Engineer, GLBC, 26 June 1980.
Morales, Jorge, Manager, Word Processing Systems, MBT, 11 July 1980.
Morgan, Cricket, Supervisor, Word Processing Systems, Purdue University, 21 April, 21 July, and 28 July 1980.
Murchie, William D., Director, Bureau of Management and Services, ISBH, 31 July 1980.
Romano, Frank, Executive Development Center, IBM, 1 April 1980.
Roy, Douglas, Network Distribution Services, MBT, 13 Aug. 1980.
Ruddy, Elizabeth J., Executive Administrator, MDSI, 26 June and 1 July 1980.
Simonenko, Sam, General Administrative Assistant in Charge of Dictation Network and Word Processing, MBT, 13 Aug. 1980.
Sonzogni, William C., Director, Environmental Studies, GLBC, 26 June 1980.
Sullivan, Rose Ann C., Water Resources Engineer, GLBC, 26 June 1980.

We interviewed these people at work in locations in the eastern third of the country. We consider this a representative sample for two reasons: (1) The interviewees represent a wide range of organizational settings—large and small; business, industry, government, and the professions; (2) Results from this sample have been confirmed by interviews with other systems users and word processing personnel in Arizona, California, Connecticut, Delaware, Hawaii, New York, and Texas.

Abbreviation Key to Companies in Which More than One Interview Was Conducted

GLBC United States Great Lakes Basin Commission
 3475 Plymouth Rd.
 Ann Arbor, MI 48106

ISBH Indiana State Board of Health
 1330 W. Michigan St.
 Indianapolis, IN 46206

MBT Michigan Bell Telephone Company
 Bell Building
 Detroit, MI 48226
 Regional Offices: Livonia and Southfield

MDSI Manufacturing Data Systems International
 4251 Plymouth Rd.
 Ann Arbor, MI 48106

SFI State Farm Insurance
 2550 Northwestern Ave.
 W. Lafayette, IN 47906

Appendix B
Questions on Structured Interview Form

1. What are your main job responsibilities?
2. How do you divide your work time in terms of various tasks?
3. What percent of your time is spent writing or dictating?
4. What kinds of communications do you typically write, and what percent of your writing time is devoted to each?
5. What kinds of communications do you typically dictate, and what percent of your dictating time is devoted to each?
6. Describe the process you go through when you dictate from the time you decide to dictate a communication to the time you sign it.
7. Are your dictated communications usually first-time-final, or do you change them and have them retyped? If you do, what kinds of changes do you typically make?
8. How long does it take between the time you dictate and the time you get your communication back for reviewing or signing?
9. How does dictation differ from your other writing?
10. What specific skills do you need to dictate?
11. If you were going to teach someone to dictate very efficiently, that is, to produce communications which were effective the first time around, what tips would you give?

Appendix C
The Process of Dictation [1]

ACTIVITY	TYPE OF COMMUNICATION			
	Draft	First-time Final	Adapted Form	Record
Pre-dictation Planning				
Choosing Dictation Option	*****	*****	*****	*****
Clarifying Purpose	*****	*****	****	****
Remembering; Assembling References	*****	*****	****	****
Attending to Long-term Audiences	****	*****	***	*
Attending to Short-term Audiences	***	*****	*****	***
Attending to Content	*****	*****	****	*****
Organizing	*****	*****	****	****
Making Notes	*****	****	****	**
Making Outlines	*****	*	*	—
Distinguishing Between Speaking and Writing	****	*****	***	—
Translating During Dictation				
Following Equipment Instructions	*****	*****	*****	*****
Giving Directions to Short-term Audience	***	*****	*****	**
Planning Paragraphs	****	****	*	—
Planning Sentences	****	*****	***	*
Planning Sentences	****	*****	***	*

Appendix C

Planning Phrases/Words Structures	****	*****	****	*
Adding New Information	***	*****	***	***
Correcting Tape	*	*****	*****	*
Attaching Notes for Typist	***	***	*****	*

Reviewing: Revising/Editing/Correcting

On Tape	*	*****	*****	*
On Draft	*****	—	*	—
On Final Copy	***	***	***	—
Of Content	*****	***	****	—
Of Organization	****	*	***	—
Of Style	**	***	**	—
By Dictator	****	***	***	—
By Typist	***	****	***	—
By Others	****	*	**	—

Key:
- ***** Essential
- **** Important
- *** Routine
- ** Sometimes Omitted
- * Often Omitted
- — Unnecessary

Appendix D
Segment of Edited First Draft, Summary of Actions[2]

#3.11

STANDING COMMITTEE ON RESEARCH AND DEVELOPMENT ← Proper name for Committee?

Traverse City, Michigan
June 10, 1980 ← OK?

(Meeting Held during Workshop on NOAA's 5-Year Plan for G.L. Research, Development and Monitoring)

SUMMARY OF ACTIONS

1. A brief meeting of the committee was held during the NOAA-sponsored workshop on the five year plan for Great Lakes Research, Development and Monitoring. Since this workshop addressed one of the long-range objectives of the R&D Committee, and since it is chaired by the current A&D Committee chairman, Dr. Beeton, all members of the R&D Committee were invited to attend. In the way of a brief summary of this workshop, several major research needs were recurrent throughout the workshop:

(a) basic scientific research on the processes and fates of contaminants in the Great Lakes system;

(continued on next page)

Appendix D

(b)/ the ~~need for~~ *quantitative* ⓓ ~~get a better handle~~ *information* on ⓓ ⊕ *the* economics associated with water ⓢ ✓
pollution /(i.e.,/ the need to quantify costs and benefits)⊕; ⊕ /

(c) the urgent need for additional information on ᵒ✓/ human health risks from   <u>Omitted</u>
the

```
          Annotation Key
   /  -  tape stop
   i  -  instructions to secretary
   sp-   spelling direction
   v  -  sound pause
   +  -  pause filler--ah, throat clear
   ^  -  punctuation direction
   o  -  secretary omitted
   ∅  -  secretary changed
   ⊕  -  secretary added
   x  -  dictator's rewording
```

Appendix E
Segment of Final Copy, Summary of Actions

STANDING COMMITTEE ON RESEARCH AND DEVELOPMENT

Traverse City, Michigan
June 10, 1980

(Meeting Held during Workshop on NOAA's
5-Year Plan for Great Lakes Research, Development and Monitoring)

SUMMARY OF ACTIONS

1. A brief meeting of the committee was held during the NOAA-sponsored workshop on Great Lakes research, development and monitoring. Since the NOAA workshop addressed one of the objectives of the R&D Committee, namely long-term planning for research, all members of the R&D Committee were invited to attend. In the way of a brief summary of the NOAA workshop, several major research needs were recurrent:

   (a) basic scientific research on the processes and fates of contaminants in the Great Lakes system;

   (b) more quantitative information on the economics associated with water pollution (i.e., the need to quantify costs and benefits);

   (c) the urgent need for additional information on human health risks from contaminants found in the lakes;

   (d) comprehensive research programs which treat the lakes as an ecosystem (the need to look at the "big picture" was stressed, and the need to identify interactions, such as the need to look at point and nonpoint control programs concurrently or how phosphorus control programs may affect toxic substances inputs, was identified; how institutions can be more effective by taking an ecosystem approach was also identified);

(e) research on how monitoring and data storage can be done more economically and effectively.

2. It was observed that no attempt was made at the <u>NOAA workshop</u> to analyze research needs with the actual five year federal plan. At the time of the conference, the 1980-1985 plan was not available. It is important that Congress receive information on what needs are being inadequately addressed, not just the needs. Consequently, the R&D Committee may wish to address this problem.

Appendix F
Sample of First-time-final Letter[3]

(Note clipped to signed letter.)

Add Hank Tripp to the cc list

ANNALS OF THE HISTORY OF COMPUTING

Editor-in-Chief, Bernard A. Galler
Assistant Editor-in-Chief, Nancy Stern

Reply to:

Computing Center
University of Michigan
1075 Beal Avenue
Ann Arbor, MI 48109
313/764-9595

June 4, 1980

Professor Fritz L. Bauer
Institute fur Informatik
Arcisstrasse 21
D-8000 Munich
GERMANY

Dear Fritz,

It was a great shock to learn about Klaus Samelson. I remember very well the good times and the arguments we had over ALGOL 58. I know especially that you and he were very close colleagues, and I'm sure that he will be greatly missed. —— Omitted for me that

When Heinz Zemanek told me about Klaus, we discussed the preparation of a memorial article for the Annals. Heinz suggested that you would be the appropriate person to write such a memorial, if you would be willing to do so. We have now had several such memorials in the Annals, and you could get an idea

Appendix F

⌀ of what ᵛmight be appropriate from them ͺ /Please let me know ᵛif
you ᵛare willing to do this./
                        ^
                                    Sincerely,

                                    Bernie

                                    Bernard A. Galler
                                         ⊕   ⊕

⊕ BAG:kls

cc: Nancy Stern
    Heinz Zemanek
    Mondy Dana
     i /

```
           Annotation Key
    / - tape stop
    i - instructions to secretary
    sp- spelling direction
    v - sound pause
    + - pause filler--ah, throat clear
    ^ - punctuation direction
    o - secretary omitted
    ⌀ - secretary changed
    ⊕ - secretary added
    x - dictator's rewording
```

Appendix G
Flower and Hayes' Model of Composing in Writing*

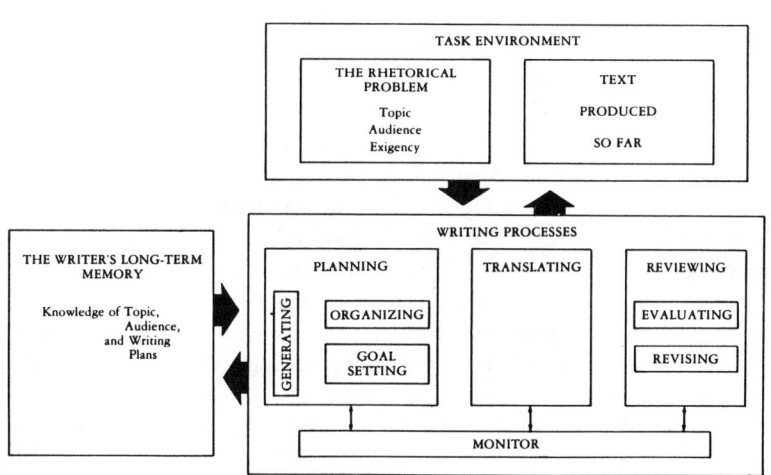

*From Linda Flower and John R. Hayes, "A Cognitive Process Theory of Writing," *College Composition and Communication* 32 (Dec. 1981): 370. Copyright 1981 by NCTE; reprinted with permission.[4]

Appendix H
Using Audio Mail: An Assignment

Situation

You are the branch manager of the local Student Credit Union, SCU, a nationwide lending institution. The graphic design department of SCU is sponsoring a contest for employees: a competition to design a new logo. The only stipulations are that the design incorporate (1) the initials SCU, (2) a circle to symbolize over 75 years of continuous service, (3) a square to represent a solid financial basis, and (4) a triangle to stand for the institution's motto, "Service, Trust, and Understanding." After much doodling, you create what you think is an award-winning design. Since the deadline for entries is tomorrow at noon, you call the design department to describe your entry. When the phone rings, you hear, "Hello. Student Credit Union. This is Lynn Porter, design department. Our office is closed for the day. At the tone, please leave your message." (You forgot that the design center, located almost 800 miles away, is in a different time zone!) You decide to take advantage of the department's audio mail system and leave a message, hoping Lynn understands your reason for calling and reproduces your design accurately. The $500 for the winning design will certainly come in handy!

Assignment

Assume the role of the branch manager and do the following:

1. Create a logo incorporating the initials SCU, a circle, a square, and a triangle.

2. Report to the writing lab today or tomorrow at the scheduled time to tape the audio mail message for Lynn Porter. (Bring a copy of your design and a brief outline for your message with you; however, do not write out detailed directions beforehand.)

3. After recording your message, you will be asked to listen to a classmate's audio mail message. Try to reproduce his or her logo and evaluate the completeness and clarity of that audio mail message. Consider the following questions: How clear and complete is your classmate's audio mail message? What parts of the message are particularly helpful in re-creating the design? What important information did your classmate omit, either for the design or the message as a whole? (Be sure to note your classmate's name and your name on the logo you draw.)

4. Be prepared to discuss your experience with audio mail at the next class meeting. Please bring these three things to class: (1) your own logo design, (2) the design you sketched while listening to your classmate's tape, and (3) your evaluation of your classmate's audio mail message.

Appendix I
Audio Mail: A User's Guide

Louis Mertes, in his article, "Doing Your Office Over—Electronically," says of audio mail: "At first, bank employees confronted with a recorded message often felt inclined to hang up."[5] He suggests that users must be educated about how a new communication system works and what its advantages are. Many organizations prepare user's guides to teach new employees this kind of information. Your assignment is to prepare such a guide for users of audio mail.

Writer: You are technical writer for Student Credit Union (SCU), responsible for preparing training manuals for personnel.

Audience: Prepare your guide for employees at SCU who are unfamiliar with audio mail. Explain what it is, how it works, why it should be used.

Assignment: Prepare a two-page user's guide for audio mail. Describe the system, explain the process, and give whatever other information you believe is essential for using audio mail systems effectively. Incorporate features that make such a guide easy to use and understand: clear organization, useful format, etc. Your goal is to teach callers not to hang up at the sound of a recorded message but to follow your procedures and accomplish the original purpose for the call.

Bring a draft of your "User's Guide for Audio Mail" to class next time for peer evaluation.

Appendix J
Students' Responses to Unit on Audio Mail

After students taped audio mail messages and wrote user's guides, they responded to these five statements, where SA = strongly agree, A = agree, U = undecided, D = disagree, and SD = strongly disagree. The results are recorded as number of students responding in a given category; there were 20 students in the class.

	SA	A	U	D	SD
1. During this unit, I learned about communication systems I'd never heard of before.	1	11	2	6	
2. I expect to use such systems on my job some day.	4	11	3	2	
3. I particularly enjoyed learning about how audio mail systems work.	1	12	6	1	
4. Leaving an audio mail message helped me understand the process better and to write a better user's guide.	6	14			
5. In the future when I call someone and hear, "At the tone, please leave a message," I'll put into practice what I learned in this unit.	8	11		1	

Appendix K
Sources for Teaching Dictation[6]

Billett, Nancy J. "Hints for Effective Dictation." *Business Education Forum* 33 (Nov. 1978): 15–16.

Boris, E. Z. "Pairing of Business Communication and Word Processing Classes." *ABCA Bulletin* 39 (Sept. 1976): 6.

Casady, M. J. "How to Teach Machine Dictation." *ABCA Bulletin* 43 (June 1980): 23–29.

Gonzalez, Jean. *The Complete Guide to Effective Dictation*. Boston, MA: Kent, 1980.

Gould, John D. "How Experts Dictate." *Journal of Experimental Psychology: Human Perception and Performance* 4 (Nov. 1978): 648–61.

Hennington, Jo Ann. "Teaching the Dictator to Dictate." *Business Education World* 61 (Nov.–Dec. 1980): 21–22.

Kruk, Leonard B. "Word Processing and Its Implications for Business Communications Courses." *Journal of Business Communication* 15 (Spring 1978): 9–18.

Lewis, Stephen D. "Dictation Skill for Today's Offices." *Business Education Forum* 35 (Oct. 1980): 12–14.

Liggett, Sarah. "Preparing Students for a New Mode of Business Communication: Dictation for Word Processing Systems." In *People and Information: The Intermix for Successful Communication: Proceedings of 1981 National Conference of the American Business Communication Association*, pp. 207–21. Urbana, IL: ABCA, 1981.

Matthews, Anne L., and Patricia Moody. *The Letter Clinic: How to Dictate*. Cincinnati, OH: Southwestern, 1982.

Mayer, Kenneth R., and Bella Clinkscale. "Identification and Validation of Dictation Competencies." *The Delta Pi Epsilon Journal* 22 (Apr. 1980): 15–27.

Rogers, Florence. "Dictation: The Weak Link in Word Processing Production." *The Personnel Administrator* 24 (Sept. 1979): 25–28, 34+.

Schrag, Adele F. *How To Dictate*. New York: McGraw, 1981.

Appendix L
McCoy's Memo, Used in Dictation Assignment

To: Sarah Liggett, English 420 Instructor

From: Jim McCoy, Placement Counselor

Date: April 3, 1981

Subject: <u>Class Presentation on Locating Summer Jobs</u>

In our phone conversation last Wednesday, you asked me to address your business writing class on tips for locating summer jobs. For my presentation to be effective, I need the following information about your class and scheduled meeting:

* Students' classification by school and semester
* Students' major area of study
* Number who've held summer jobs related to major
* Major area of interest--business, industry, government, education

Once you've confirmed your class schedule, let me know the date, time and place your class meets. I will be out of town the second week in April.

I look forward to speaking with your class.

Appendix M
Guide to Planning Effective Dictation, Completed by Students in Response to the Memo Assignment

TO: Identify the Audience
1. The short-term audience will transcribe your dictated memo. What special considerations must be made throughout the dictation for this audience?
   signal format, spelling, punctuation, fling

2. The long-term audience will act on or be affected by the information the memo contains. List the name(s) below; star anyone's name who should receive a copy of the memo.
   * *address to Jim McCoy, Placement center*
   * *Jeanne Halpern, Director of Business Writing*
   other business writing teachers, students

FROM: Identify the Dictator
1. Name
   Sarah Piggott, Business Writing Instructor

2. Organization
   English Dept., Purdue University

DATE: Determine the Date
What is the appropriate date to issue the memo?
   today's date

SUBJECT: Specify the Subject
The subject line should state the topic and suggest the purpose of the memo.
   Information for the Summer Job Presentation

Appendix M

DETERMINE PURPOSE

1. What is the context, problem, or issue of concern to the organization?
   McCoy needs date, time, place of meeting, & class info

2. Does the memo respond to previous communications on the issue? If so, what were you asked to do?
   McCoy's memo 4/3/81 Get info & set date

3. What do you wish to accomplish by sending this memo?
   Give McCoy info on meeting & class

GATHER INFORMATION AND GENERATE IDEAS

What materials and information do you need to get or give to accomplish your purpose? List them here.

② 23 in class ③ 12 MGMT ④ 5 Srs. -- don't want summer jobs
5 SUPV   10 Jrs. ⑥ held related jobs before
① april 20 - 3:30   3 HUM   8 Soph.
Rm 2 HH   3 CFS   ⑤ Interested in bus., indust. & ₮ ✱ ✱
⑦ Class has already written resumes & application letters

SELECT AND ORGANIZE MATERIALS

1. Number the information listed above from most to least important or general to specific, based on what your audience most wants to know.

2. Determine an appropriate closing. If an action ending is needed, what do you want your audience to do? How? Make it easy and provide a stimulus for action if appropriate. Otherwise, use a courteous ending.
   If date not OK, call 3/1/15   Thanks!

3. Review the information you've selected. Star any information that belongs in an attachment rather than the body of the memo. Make a key word outline to reflect the content and order of your memo. *① 4/20/81 3:30 Rm 2 HH   3) Bus. & indust.; 5 related jobs*
   ② 23 students -- class info from above
   ④ date, ok, thanks

ATTEND TO STYLE AND FORMAT

1. What headings, spacing, special format or attachments would complement your memo?
   Give class info in chart form

2. What tone is appropriate for your purpose and audience?
   Informal, friendly

Appendix N
Personnel Director's Memo, Used in Dictation Experiment

TO: Your Name, Recruiter

FROM: Nathan Toothman, Personnel Director

DATE: April 10, 1981

SUBJECT: <u>Interviewing Prospective Trainees</u>

Currently, the plant has openings on the production line in quality control and shipping. We have to hire qualified people to begin our training program. I have scheduled you to conduct screening interviews for three applicants on Tuesday afternoon, April 14. Please use the following guidelines.

Based on your judgment of the applicants' potential, you may recommend that we hire none, 1, 2 or all 3 applicants. When interviewing,

   *Consider skills, work experience, education
    and interpersonal skills carefully.

   *Remember that it costs the company $250 to
    train an employee. We have to reduce our turn-
    over rate by hiring prospective long-term workers.

I need your detailed recommendations on why or why not to hire each of the interviewees by Thursday, April 16. Please send a copy of your recommendations to Doris Hoover, training director, as well. Call me if you have any questions: 463-3362.

Notes

1. The New Technologies Are Changing Written Communication

1. Edmund J. Farrell, *English, Education, and the Electronic Revolution* (Urbana, IL: NCTE, 1967), p. 68.
2. Edward P. J. Corbett, "What Is Being Revived?" *College Composition and Communication* 18 (Oct. 1967): 172.
3. For McLuhan's observations on electronic media, see Marshall McLuhan, *Understanding Media: The Extensions of Man* (New York: McGraw, 1965); Marshall McLuhan and Quentin Fiore, *The Medium is the Massage* (New York: Bantam, 1967). For background on the Dartmouth Seminars, see John Dixon, *Growth Through English* (London: Oxford Univ. Pr., 1967); Herbert J. Muller, *The Uses of English* (New York: Holt, 1967); and James R. Squire and Roger K. Applebee, *Teaching English in the United Kingdom: A Comparative Study* (Urbana, IL: NCTE, 1969), pp. 3–17.
4. Pioneering books and articles on the use of electronic media in English classrooms include William D. Boutwell, *Using Mass Media in the Schools* (New York: Appleton, 1962); Neil Postman, *Television and the Teaching of English* (New York: Appleton, 1961); Marion C. Sheridan, Harold H. Owen, Jr., Ken Macrorie, and Fred Marcus, *The Motion Picture and the Teaching of English* (New York: Appleton, 1965). More recent publications include Harold M. Foster, *The New Literacy: The Language of Film and Television* (Urbana, IL: NCTE, 1979); and David L. Stoeoff, "Four Models for Viewing Television and Their Implications for Educational Planning," *Education Technology* 20 (Oct. 1980): 23–30. For publications on adapting computer technology to the English classroom, see Paula Reed Nancarrow, Donald Ross, and Lillian Bridwell, *Word Processors and the Writing Process: An Annotated Bib-*

liography (Minneapolis: English Dept., Univ. of Minnesota, 1982); Shavaun M. Wall and Nancy E. Taylor, "Using Interactive Computer Programs in Teaching Higher Conceptual Skills: An Approach to Instruction in Writing," *Educational Technology* 22 (Feb. 1982): 13–17; and William Wresch, "Computers in English Class, Finally Beyond Grammar and Spelling Drills," *College English* 44 (Sept. 1982): 483–90.
5. Lester Faigley and Thomas P. Miller, "What We Learn from Writing on the Job," *College English* 44 (Oct. 1982): 561.
6. Faigley and Miller, p. 569.
7. Alvin Toffler, *The Third Wave* (New York: Bantam, 1980), p. 139.
8. Sheldon E. Brucker, "Energy and the Communication Revolution," *Personnel Administrator* 26 (June 1981): 23.
9. Faigley and Miller, pp. 559–560.
10. Martha H. Radar and Alan P. Wunsch, "A Survey of Communication Practices of Business School Graduates by Job Category and Undergraduate Major," *Journal of Business Communication* 17 (Summer 1980): 36.
11. Frederick Williams, *The Communications Revolution* (Beverly Hills, CA: Sage, 1982), pp. 55–56.
12. For example, on 28 January 1983, at Purdue University, a nationwide teleconference, "Facing the Challenges of Productivity in America," was offered as part of the university's division of independent study. The teleconference, sponsored by the National University Teleconference Network, connected 50 locations. More examples of how teleconferencing is used in educational settings are presented by F. Williams, pp. 215–26.
13. For an overview of teleconferencing in business, see John Perham, "Business' New Communication Tool," *Dun's Review* 117 (Feb. 1981): 80–82; and Patrick Lee, "Bouncing Around a Good Idea: Satellite Videoconferencing," *California Business* (Feb. 1982), pp. 40–41, 60, 79.
14. Lee, p. 41, 79; Hanley Miller, "Teleconferencing," *Computerworld* 15 (28 Sept. 1981): 27.
15. Louis H. Mertes, "Doing Your Office Over—Electronically," *Harvard Business Review* 59 (Mar.–Apr. 1981): 133.
16. Mertes, "Doing Your Office Over," p. 127.
17. Louis H. Mertes, "The Professional Environment in the 21st Century," *Computerworld* 15 (1 Sept. 1981): 34.
18. Christopher Byron, "Fighting the Paper Chase," *Time*, 23 Nov. 1981, pp. 66–67; Jeffrey Rothfeder, "Electronic Mail Delivers the Executive Message," *Personal Computing* (June 1982), pp. 32–40, 118; and "Electronic Mail Speeds Appeals Process for Third Circuit," *Word Processing Systems* (Oct. 1979), pp. 16–18.
19. Interview with Holly Rahbar, Systems Marketing and Training, Conti-

nental Illinois Bank, Chicago, 22 Apr. 1983. Ms. Rahbar, whose background is in English Education, demonstrated the training that professionals and managers receive to use the multiple functions of the bank's electronic mail system.
20. William Zinsser, *Writing with a Word Processor* (New York: Harper, 1983), describes in detail this arduous learning experience.
21. For a general description of the Phoenix system, see "Phoenix Improves Productivity with WP Operations," *Word Processing Systems* (June 1980), pp. 14–17.
22. Elizabeth J. Ruddy, Executive Assistant to the President, Manufacturing Data Systems International, Ann Arbor, MI: Interviewed by Jeanne W. Halpern, 26 June 1980.
23. "WPS Measures Dictation Usage," *Word Processing Systems* (Feb. 1980), p. 22.
24. For confirmation of the widespread use of dictation systems by professionals, see, for example: *An Attorney's Guide to Modern Office Dictation*, published by Dictaphone Corporation for the American Bar Association, Committee on Economics of Law Practice, 1971; "How a Texas Hospital Copes with Dictation Processing," *The Office* 92 (Sept. 1980): 22; and "Dictation to Cut Correspondence Costs," *The Accountant* 183 (31 July 1980): 186.
25. John D. Gould, "Experiments on Composing Letters: Some Facts, Some Myths, and Some Observations," in *Cognitive Processes in Writing*, ed. Lee W. Gregg and Erwin R. Steinberg (Hillsdale, NJ: Lawrence Erlbaum, 1980), p. 102.
26. See for example: "Dictation and Electronic Typing Step Up Efficiency at FAA Facility in Atlanta," *The Office* 93 (Feb. 1981): 19–20.
27. Howard Gardner, "On Becoming a Dictator," *Psychology Today* 14 (Dec. 1980): 19.
28. Walter J. Ong, *Interfaces of the Word: Studies in the Evolution of Consciousness and Culture* (Ithaca, NY: Cornell Univ. Pr., 1977), p. 87.
29. "Dictation Today: Voices of the Users," *Modern Office Procedures* (March 1979), p. 70.
30. Gould, p. 101.
31. For example, the Indiana State Board of Health in Indianapolis and Michigan Bell Telephone in Detroit keep daily, weekly, and monthly line-counts of dictated/word processed documents.

2. *The New Systems Require New Composing Strategies*

1. For a more detailed analysis of Sonzogni's composing process, see Jeanne W. Halpern, "Paper Voices: How Dictation and Word Process-

ing Are Changing the Way College Graduates Write," ERIC, Document ED 203 318, pp. 13–18.
2. The only exception was William Murchie, Director of the Bureau of Management and Services, Indiana State Board of Health, who had introduced the department-wide system in 1977 and who was eager to show that he used it. At age 64, however, Murchie could not seem to break his lifetime habit of writing all communications in longhand, so he wrote and then dictated them. When asked why he bothered to dictate, Murchie said he "wanted to set a good example."
3. Ong, *Interfaces*, p. 42.
4. For an explanation of the cognitive process model of writing developed by Linda Flower and John R. Hayes, see "A Cognitive Process Theory of Writing," *College Composition and Communication* 32 (Dec. 1981): 365–87; and John R. Hayes and Linda Flower, "Identifying the Organization of Writing Processes," in *Cognitive Processes in Writing*, ed. Lee W. Gregg and Erwin R. Steinberg (Hillsdale, NJ: Lawrence Erlbaum, 1980), pp. 10–21.
5. There are, however, exceptions. At one of the three word processing centers which serve the entire city government of Phoenix, Arizona, transcriptionists have notebooks which contain sheets showing the stylistic, mechanical, and format features specific dictators prefer, and also frequently dictated names, addresses, and difficult-to-spell words. This particular center, of course, serves only the Mayor, City Council, and top administrators: Site tour, Phoenix Center, 14 Oct. 1981, and interview with Vicky Miel, Manager, Phoenix Word Processing Center.
6. J. C. Mathes and Dwight Stevenson, *Designing Technical Reports: Writing for Audiences in Organizations* (Indianapolis: Bobbs-Merrill, 1976), pp. 9–23. Mathes and Stevenson use the word "immediate" for what we call "tertiary."
7. Martin Joos, *The Five Clocks* (New York: Harcourt, 1961), pp. 20–23. Example originally presented by Charles Carpenter Fries, *The Structure of English* (New York: Harcourt, 1952), p. 50.
8. Joos, p. 34.
9. Joos, p. 37.
10. John C. Schafer, "The Linguistic Analysis of Spoken and Written Texts," in *Exploring Speaking-Writing Relationships: Connections and Contrasts*, ed. Barry M. Kroll and Roberta J. Vann (Urbana, IL: NCTE, 1981), pp. 22–31.
11. Gardner, p. 14.
12. Gardner, pp. 14–15. Interviewee Timothy Monteith, Water Resources Engineer at the Great Lakes Basin Commission, structured interview, 26 June 1980, explained his preference for dictating drafts this way: "I

can talk faster than I can write. When I write, I stop all the time to check spelling and words." Monteith's observation and those of other interviewees suggest that some writers prefer dictation in drafting because it allows them to *avoid* editing interferences which "interrupt other processes," including translation (Hayes and Flower, p. 19).
13. George Heighway, Director, Division of Health Facilities, Indiana State Board of Health, from structured interview, conducted 31 July 1980.
14. Pamela Graves, Claims Service Specialist, State Farm Insurance, from interview, conducted 29 Aug. 1980.
15. *Attorney's Guide to Modern Office Dictation*, p. 11. We encountered only one interviewee who, in using the record-keeping function, dictated his observations in a casual way. Jack Manes, former Vice-President for Human Resources, Manufacturing Data Systems International, reported in a structured interview on 1 July 1980 that he attends meetings, observes group dynamics, and, when he has a free minute in a private place, records his observations on a pocket recorder; his secretary then transcribes and files them for later use in drafting professional articles.
16. Lee Odell, "Teachers of Composition and Needed Research in Discourse Theory," *College Composition and Communication* 30 (Feb. 1979): 41; C. H. Knoblauch, "Intentionality in the Writing Process: A Case Study," *College Composition and Communication* 31 (May 1980): 153–59; Thomas Pearsall, *Audience Analysis for Technical Writers* (Beverly Hills, CA: Glenco Pr., 1969); and Janet Emig, "Writing as a Mode of Learning," *College Composition and Communication* 28 (May 1977): 123–24.
17. Gould, p. 113; Peter Elbow, *Writing Without Teachers* (New York: Oxford Univ. Pr., 1973), pp. 3–11.
18. Charles K. Stallard, "An Analysis of the Writing of Good Student Writers," *Research in the Teaching of English* 8 (Summer 1974): 217.
19. Emig, pp. 122–28. Sondra Perl, "Understanding Composing," *College Composition and Communication* 31 (Dec. 1980): 363–69.
20. Bonnie J. F. Meyer, "Reading Research and the Composition Teacher: The Importance of Plans," *College Composition and Communication* 33 (Feb. 1982): 37.
21. In a related technological area, Judith Stein and JoAnne Yates, "Electronic Mail: How Will It Change Office Communication? Can Managers Use It Effectively?" in *Information Systems and Business Communication*, ed. Alfred B. Williams, (Urbana, IL: ABCA, forthcoming), describe the unusual importance of these functions in composing messages on electronic mail systems.

22. Gould, p. 102.
23. Stallard, p. 215; Perl, pp. 363–69.
24. Ann Matsuhashi, "Pausing and Planning: The Tempo of Written Discourse Production," *Research in the Teaching of English* 15 (May 1981): 113–34. Matsuhashi closely analyzed pauses in the composing behavior of four skilled high school writers; her research showed that the more abstract or complex the sentence, the longer the planning pause.
25. Hayes and Flower, p. 15.
26. Hayes and Flower, p. 16; Matsuhashi, pp. 129–30.
27. Brian Cambourne, "Oral and Written Relationships: A Reading Perspective," in *Exploring Speaking-Writing Relationships: Connections and Contrasts*, ed. Barry M. Kroll and Roberta J. Vann (Urbana, IL: NCTE, 1981), p. 96, refers to "patterns . . . firmly established in long-term memory"; Linda Flower, "Writer-Based Prose: A Cognitive Basis for Problems in Writing," *College English* 41 (Sept. 1979): 35, refers to "semantic memory"; E. D. Hirsch, Jr., *The Philosophy of Composition* (Chicago: Univ. of Chicago Pr., 1977), pp. 10, 150–57, refers to "linguistic forms" which move from reading through memory to writing.
28. Jerome Bruner, Jacqueline J. Goodnow, and George A. Austin, *A Study of Thinking* (New York: Wiley, 1956), p. 54; Carroll C. Arnold, "Oral Rhetoric, Rhetoric, and Literature," in *Contemporary Rhetoric*, ed. Douglas Ehninger (Glenview, IL: Scott, Foresman, 1972), p. 64.
29. Flower, "Writer-Based Prose," pp. 34–36, and Flower and Hayes, "A Cognitive Process Theory," pp. 371–72, have begun to explore this topic, bringing to bear their background in cognitive psychology; in "Writer-Based Prose," Flower lists several useful references. Hirsch, pp. 116–18, 153–54, also discusses memory, though mainly at the sentence level. Richard Young and Patricia Sullivan, "Why Write: A Reconsideration," in *Classical Rhetoric and Modern Discourse: Essays in Honor of Edward P. J. Corbett*, ed. Robert J. Connors, Lisa Ede, and Andrea Lunsford (Carbondale, IL: Southern Illinois Univ. Pr., forthcoming), also discuss relationships between memory and writing.
30. Walter J. Ong, *Orality and Literacy: The Technologizing of the Word* (New York: Methuen, 1982), p. 79.
31. David R. Olson, "Writing: The Divorce of the Author from the Text," in *Exploring Speaking-Writing Relationships: Connections and Contrasts*, ed. Barry M. Kroll and Roberta J. Vann (Urbana, IL: NCTE, 1981), pp. 99–110.
32. Edward P. J. Corbett, *Classical Rhetoric for the Modern Student*, 2d ed. (New York: Oxford Univ. Pr., 1971), p. 38.
33. Richard C. Anderson, "Schema-directed Processes in Language Com-

prehension," in *The Psychology of Written Communication*, ed. James Hartley (London: Kogan Page, 1980), pp. 33–37; and Rand J. Spiro, "Remembering Information from Text: Theoretical and Empirical Issues Concerning the 'State of Schema' Reconstruction Hypothesis," in *Schooling and the Acquisition of Knowledge*, ed. Richard C. Anderson, Rand J. Spiro, and William E. Montague (Hillsdale, NJ: Lawrence Erlbaum, 1977), pp. 137–65.
34. Hayes and Flower, pp. 10, 13.
35. Linda S. Flower and John R. Hayes, "The Dynamics of Composing: Making Plans and Juggling Constraints," in *Cognitive Processes in Writing*, ed. Lee W. Gregg and Erwin R. Steinberg (Hillsdale, NJ: Lawrence Erlbaum, 1980), pp. 31–50.
36. For example: Don Rogers, *Executive Dictation Cookbook* (Atlanta: Lanier, 1979); *Word Processing Users' Manual* (Phoenix: City of Phoenix, 1981); and *Word Processing Originator's Manual* (Indianapolis: Indiana State Board of Health, 1980).
37. Arthur N. Applebee, *Tradition and Reform in the Teaching of English: A History* (Urbana, IL: NCTE, 1974), p. 160. Applebee calls reading, writing, listening, and speaking the "four fundamental language arts," but he also notes the insecure position of speaking in the group.
38. Lev S. Vygotsky, *Thought and Language*, ed. and trans. Eugenia Hanfmann and Gertrude Vakar (Cambridge, MA: MIT Pr., 1962); Aleksandr R. Luria and F. I. Yudovich, *Speech and the Development of Mental Processes in the Child*, ed. Joan Simon (Baltimore: Penguin, 1971); James W. Gibson et al., "A Quantitative Examination of Differences and Similarities in Written and Spoken Messages," *Speech Monographs* 33 (Nov. 1966): 444–51.
39. James Moffett, *Teaching the Universe of Discourse* (Boston: Houghton, 1968); Robert Zoellner, "Talk-Write: A Behavioral Pedagogy for Composition," *College English* 30 (Jan. 1969): 267–320. See also Barry M. Kroll, "Developmental Relationships between Speaking and Writing," in *Exploring Speaking-Writing Relationships: Connections and Contrasts*, ed. Barry M. Kroll and Roberta J. Vann (Urbana, IL: NCTE, 1981), pp. 32–54; Terry Radcliffe, "Talk-Write Composition: A Theoretical Model Proposing the Use of Speech to Improve Writing," *Research in the Teaching of English* 6 (Fall 1972): 189–99; and Anthony Tovatt and Elbert L. Miller, "Oral-Aural-Visual Stimuli Approach to Teaching Written Composition to 9th Grade Students," ERIC, Document ED 015 204, 1967.
40. Marie E. Flatley and Gretchen Vik, "Incorporating Oral Communication and Dictation Skills in Business Writing Classes," in *Teaching Business Writing: Approaches, Plans, Pedagogy, Research*, ed. Jeanne W.

Halpern (Urbana, IL: ABCA, 1983), pp. 129–45. See also, in the same text, Herbert W. Hildebrandt, "Societal and Technological Change: Two Challenges for Research and Teaching," pp. 200–13.
41. Emig, pp. 123–24; Nancy Sommers, "Revision Strategies of Student Writers and Experienced Adult Writers," *College Composition and Communication* 31 (Dec. 1980): 378–379.
42. Kroll, p. 53, summarizes his position as follows: "When oral and written resources are systematically integrated, . . . a person can make *choices* within a flexible, organized system of voices, registers, and styles—choices which are appropriate for the purpose, audience, and context of communication."
43. Donald M. Murray, "Internal Revision: A Process of Discovery," in *Research on Composing: Points of Departure*, ed. Charles R. Cooper and Lee Odell (Urbana, IL: NCTE, 1978), p. 91.
44. Eric von Grimmenstein, Lanier representative, in his presentation to classes at Purdue University, 14 April 1981, demonstrated fast-forward scanning and described it as a technique frequently used for reviewing and revising dictated tapes.
45. We observed this procedure at the Great Lakes Basin Commission and at Purdue University, where word processing centers serve relatively small groups; at Michigan Bell and the Indiana State Board of Health, on the other hand, signs on the word processing center doors say "Keep Out."
46. Gould, pp. 103, 117.
47. Barrie Van Dyke, "On-the-Job Writing of High Level Business Executives" (Paper presented at Conference on College Composition and Communication, Washington, Mar. 1980), appendix chart.
48. Murray, p. 97.
49. Sommers, p. 380.
50. Perl, pp. 363–69.
51. Lee Odell, "Redefining 'Mature Writing'" (Unpublished paper, State Univ. of New York at Albany, 1979), pp. 19–21.
52. Hayes and Flower, pp. 16–19.
53. Gould, pp. 108–109; Van Dyke, appendix chart.
54. Until voice-activated word processing becomes a reality—and even IBM, a leader in the field, does not anticipate this before the year 2000—keyboard operators will remain essential. Although "conventional secretaries are a vanishing breed," and although many white-collar workers are showing an interest in keyboarding their own communications, word processing transcriptionists are likely to remain an essential part of collaborative message production ("The New Technology: A Key to Improving Productivity and Effectiveness in Organiza-

tional Communication and Public Relations," International Association of Business Communicators [IABC] Teleconference, 28 Jan. 1982).
55. Ong, *Interfaces*, p. 83.
56. James Hartley, "Introduction" to Part 4, in *The Psychology of Written Communication*, ed. James Hartley (London: Kogan Page, 1980), pp. 187–99; Clarence A. Ellis and Gary J. Nutt, "Office Information Systems and Computer Science," *Computing Surveys* 12 (Mar. 1980): 27–60.
57. Ong, *Interfaces*, p. 84.
58. Hayes and Flower, p. 12.
59. For example: Zoellner, pp. 310–11; James L. Collins, "Speaking, Writing, and Teaching for Meaning," in *Exploring Speaking-Writing Relationships: Connections and Contrasts*, ed. Barry M. Kroll and Roberta J. Vann (Urbana, IL: NCTE, 1981), pp. 209–11.
60. Dixon, p. 44.
61. For example: James Moffett, *Active Voice* (Montclair, NJ: Boynton/Cook, 1981), pp. 21–25; Jeanne W. Halpern and Dale Matthews, "Helping Inexperienced Writers: An Informal Discussion with Mina Shaughnessy," *English Journal* 69 (Mar. 1980): 32–37.
62. Elbow, pp. 76–116; Ken Macrorie, *Telling Writing* (Rochelle Park, NY: Hayden, 1976), pp. 63–78; Janet Callaway, "Coordinating Course Objectives with Assignments, Classroom Methods, and Evaluation Procedures," in *Teaching Business Writing: Approaches, Plans, Pedagogy, Research*, ed. Jeanne W. Halpern (Urbana, IL: ABCA, 1983), pp. 99–114.
63. James Britton et al., *The Development of Writing Abilities (11–18)* (London: Macmillan Education Ltd., 1975), p. 146.
64. Lee Odell and Dixie Goswami, "Writing in a Non-Academic Setting," *Research in the Teaching of English* 16 (Oct. 1982): 201–202.
65. This question and the next were prompted by Richard Young's comment: "if the composing process begins with the perception of a social problem and ends with changes in an audience's beliefs and behaviors, that is, if it is carried out within a rhetorical situation, then classical invention is required" (Richard E. Young, "Paradigms and Problems: Needed Research in Rhetorical Invention," in *Research on Composing: Points of Departure*, ed. Charles R. Cooper and Lee Odell [Urbana, IL: NCTE, 1978], pp. 42–43). Although the specific systems we studied are typically used to address organizational rather than social problems, many of the new systems we mention in our last chapter will be used in both organizational *and* social contexts and will combine even more obviously oral and written skills. The inclusiveness of classical rhetoric, with its attention to memory and delivery, plus the broadly

transferable insights provided by the cognitive process model, suggest that the two, together, might somehow move us away from what Richard Larson suggested was our rather narrow research focus on school or literary writing and toward a broader view of verbal communication in the larger society (Richard L. Larson, "Structure and Form in Non-Fiction Prose," in *Teaching Composition: 10 Bibliographical Essays*, ed. Gary Tate [Fort Worth, TX: Texas Christian Univ. Pr., 1976], pp. 45–71). Discussing Corbett's work on classical rhetoric, Larson noted that it encourages the writer to adapt his ideas to a particular audience, occasion, *and* set of circumstances (pp. 50–51), adaptations which, according to our research, seem especially germane to the use of the new systems.

66. Janice Lauer, "Toward a Metatheory of Heuristic Procedures," *College Composition and Communication* 30 (Oct. 1979): 248–69.
67. Anne Ruggles Gere, "A Cultural Perspective on Talking and Writing," in *Exploring Speaking-Writing Relationships: Connections and Contrasts*, ed. Barry M. Kroll and Roberta J. Vann (Urbana, IL: NCTE, 1981), pp. 119–20.
68. Corbett, "What Is Being Revived?" p. 172.

3. Teachers Can Use Research about the New Systems in Freshman and Advanced Composition Classes

1. W. Ross Winterowd, "Transferable and Local Writing Skills," *Journal of Advanced Composition* 1 (Spring 1980): 1–3.
2. See for example: Laurence Behrens and Leonard J. Rosen, eds., *Writing and Reading Across the Curriculum* (Boston: Little, Brown, 1982). Chapter 7, "The Age of Computers—And Beyond," contains several essays that are likely to spark lively class discussions on the effects of computer technology on writing.
3. McLuhan and Fiore, p. 69.
4. June O. Ferrill discusses these strategies in relation to class preparation of a job description manual for an industrial firm. See "Devising New Courses for New Clientele," in *Teaching Business Writing: Approaches, Plans, Pedagogy, Research*, ed. Jeanne W. Halpern (Urbana, IL: ABCA, 1983), pp. 52–65.
5. Olson, p. 106. See also Flower and Hayes, "The Dynamics of Composing," pp. 36–40; and Hirsch, pp. 21–23.
6. In preparing to discuss differences between speaking and writing, teachers can refer to Sarah Liggett, "Relationships Between Speaking

and Writing: An Annotated Bibliography," *College Composition and Communication*, forthcoming; and Jeanne W. Halpern, "Differences Between Speaking and Writing," *College Composition and Communication*, forthcoming.
7. For brief descriptions of classical invention strategies, Burke's pentad, Rohman's pre-writing, and Pike's tagmemics, see Young, "Paradigms and Problems," pp. 35–39; for a description of inventive questioning strategies, see Richard L. Larson, "Discovery through Questioning: A Plan for Teaching Rhetorical Invention," in *Contemporary Rhetoric: A Conceptual Background with Readings*, ed. W. Ross Winterowd (New York: Harcourt, 1975), pp. 144–54.
8. Corbett, *Classical Rhetoric*; Linda Flower, *Problem-Solving Strategies for Writing* (New York: Harcourt, 1981); and Janice Lauer et al., *Four Worlds of Writing* (New York: Harper, 1981), pp. 296–327.
9. Walter J. Ong, "Literacy and Orality in Our Times," in *Profession 79* (New York: Modern Language Association, 1979), p. 3.
10. James Britton, "The Composing Processes and the Functions of Writing," in *Research on Composing: Points of Departure*, ed. Charles R. Cooper and Lee Odell (Urbana, IL: NCTE, 1978), p. 24.
11. Paul A. Eschholz, "The Prose Model Approach," in *Eight Approaches to Teaching Composition*, ed. Timothy R. Donovan and Ben W. McClelland (Urbana, IL: NCTE, 1980), p. 36.
12. James Moffett, *Teaching the Universe of Discourse*.
13. Joos, *Five Clocks*; and Schafer, pp. 22–31.
14. See for example: Tovatt and Miller, "Oral-Aural-Visual Stimuli Approach," pp. 176–89; Zoellner, pp. 267–320; Collins, pp. 198–214; Elbow, *Writing Without Teachers*; and Moffett, *Active Voice*, pp. 21–25.
15. Hirsch, p. 162.
16. Collins, pp. 198–214.
17. Elbow, pp. 76–116.
18. In our classes, we sometimes read aloud three-quarters of a short story, have students write what they consider appropriate endings, and have small groups select the "best" ending to read to the class before reading the real ending. For other ideas on listening, see: J. N. Hook and William H. Evans, *The Teaching of High School English*, 5th ed. (New York: Wiley, 1982), pp. 451–76; Sara Lunsteen, *Listening* (Urbana, IL: NCTE, 1979); Ralph G. Nichols, "Listening Is a 10-Part Skill," in Norman B. Sigband, *Communication for Management and Business* (Glenview, IL: Scott, Foresman, 1976), pp. 564–68.
19. Stein and Yates, p. 1.
20. See for example: Donald Daiker, Andrew Kerek, and Max Morenberg,

eds., *Sentence Combining and the Teaching of Writing* (Akron: Univ. of Akron Pr., 1979), and the same authors' textbook, *The Writer's Options* (New York: Harper, 1979).
21. See for example: Stephen P. Witte and Lester Faigley, "Coherence, Cohesion, and Writing Quality," *College Composition and Communication* 32 (May 1981): 189–204; Joseph M. Williams, *Style: Ten Lessons in Clarity and Grace* (Glenview, IL: Scott, Foresman, 1981); Jack Selzer, "Readability Is a Four-Letter Word," *Journal of Business Communication* 18 (Fall 1981): 21–32.
22. William Weiss, Bell Laboratories, Short Hills, NJ, IABC Teleconference.
23. Richard A. Lanham at UCLA has developed the computer-assisted HOMER program to accompany his *Revising Prose* (New York: Scribner's, 1979); and Thomas Kline at Notre Dame has developed a computer-assisted program for improving grammar and punctuation.
24. See for example: Mary H. Beaven, "Individualized Goal Setting, Self-Evaluation, and Peer Evaluation," in *Evaluating Writing: Describing, Measuring, Judging*, ed. Charles R. Cooper and Lee Odell (Urbana, IL: NCTE, 1977), pp. 135–53; Elbow, pp. 76–116; Moffett, *Active Voice*, pp. 21–26.
25. Carl Koch and James M. Brazil, *Strategies for Teaching the Composition Process* (Urbana, IL: NCTE, 1978).
26. Peter A. McWilliams, *The Word Processing Book: A Short Course in Computer Literacy* (Los Angeles: Prelude Pr., 1982), pp. 57–63.
27. Richard E. Young, "Designing Objectives for Teaching Technical Writing Courses," in *Proceedings: Program in Technical and Professional Communication* (Ann Arbor, MI, Aug. 1981), pp. 95–98.
28. Mertes, "Doing Your Office Over," pp. 127–35. Articles on uses of new communication systems appear regularly in magazines such as *Management World*, *Nation's Business*, and *The Office*.
29. Using a drawing as a springboard for writing is not an original idea. Methods books for teaching elementary through college composition suggest similar assignments to teach various writing principles—precise language, transitions, audience adaptation. This lesson is unique in its emphasis on skills needed for new communication systems within the context of traditional instruction in composition.
30. The student who dictated this memo had received training in using dictation equipment and addressing the transcriptionist, the kind of training most frequently given on the job. She had not learned strategies for adapting the pen-in-hand writing process to dictation, the kind of training we believe students need most.
31. This research is summarized at the end of this chapter and detailed by

Sarah Liggett, "Preparing Business Writing Students to Use Dictation Systems: An Experimental Study" (Ph.D. diss., Purdue University, 1982), pp. 58–78.
32. Helen M. McCabe and Estelle L. Popham, *Word Processing: A Systems Approach to the Office* (New York: Harcourt, 1977).
33. Vygotsky, p. 144.
34. C. E. Zoerner, Jr., "A Survey of Great Dictators," *ABCA Bulletin* 44 (Mar. 1981): 8.
35. Heighway, structured interview.
36. Mathes and Stevenson, pp. 9–23; Jeanne W. Halpern, "What Should We Be Teaching Students in Business Writing?" *Journal of Business Communication* 18 (Summer 1981): 43–44.
37. Knoblauch, pp. 154–55.
38. Questions adapted from Mathes and Stevenson, p. 31.
39. Meyer, p. 38.
40. Paul Fitts and Michael Posner, *Human Performance* (Belmont, CA: Brooks/Cole, 1968), p. 134.
41. Zoerner, p. 9.
42. Betty R. Ricks, "The Neglected Managerial Communication Skills," *ABCA Bulletin* 44 (Dec. 1981): 25.
43. Flower and Hayes, "Dynamics of Composing," p. 31.
44. Arnold, p. 64.
45. An informal review of 14 current business writing textbooks and training manuals indicates considerable or exclusive emphasis on the technical process of dictation—using equipment and speaking clearly—and on giving instructions to the transcriptionist.
46. We found a local sales representative of Lanier dictation equipment very cooperative; not only did he lend us new microcassette recorders for the class, but he also expertly demonstrated how to use them. After 15 minutes of instruction, students could easily operate the portable units.
47. For a sample dictation rating sheet, see Flatley and Vik, p. 142.
48. Kenneth R. Mayer and Bella G. Clinkscale, "Developing Dictation Competencies in Collegiate Business Communication Courses," in *Unfurling Communication's Colors in the 80's: Proceedings, 1980 ABCA National Conference*, ed. Sam J. Bruno (Urbana, IL: ABCA, 1980), p. 30.
49. Don Payne, "Integrating Oral and Written Business Communication," in *Exploring Speaking-Writing Relationships: Connections and Contrasts*, ed. Barry M. Kroll and Roberta J. Vann (Urbana, IL: NCTE, 1981), p. 195.
50. Flower, "Writer-Based Prose," pp. 19–37.

51. We developed this dictation unit with funds from the School of Humanities, Social Science, and Education at Purdue University. Teachers without money to pay transcriptionists can have students transcribe each other's memos.
52. Charles R. Cooper and Lee Odell, "Introduction," *Research on Composing: Points of Departure*, ed. Charles R. Cooper and Lee Odell (Urbana, IL: NCTE, 1978), p. xi.
53. Although beginning dictators may not ordinarily aim for first-time-final copy, we asked students in the experiment to dictate first-time-final memos so that we could more clearly evaluate their dictation skills. If students had been allowed to revise drafts of their memos, the resulting communications might largely have reflected revision skills—skills that students in the treatment and control groups had developed earlier in the semester. For an explanation of this assignment and further information on the experiment, see Liggett, "Preparing Business Writing Students," pp. 53–78.
54. To determine interrater reliability, we calculated Pearson-product moment correlations. The holistic scores had an interrater reliability correlation coefficient of $r = .82$ and for analytic scoring, $r = .84$. However, because we combined the scores from the two raters when we calculated analysis of variance and t-tests, the correlations could be stepped up with the use of the Spearman-Brown formula: holistic, $r = .90$; analytic, $r = .91$.

Interrater reliability for specific analytic features ranged from a high of $r = .95$ for summary to a low of $r = .40$ for grammar/mechanics. The raters' scores correlated highest on those features that could be measured most objectively. Raters tended to agree on whether a heading was correct and complete or whether a summary of recommendations appeared early in the memo. Their scores correlated less consistently on those features that could be measured more subjectively. Raters tended to agree less on whether grammatical/mechanical errors were serious or whether stylistic problems affected readability or comprehension. However, those features for which the treatment and control groups showed significant differences—heading, purpose statement, and format—have high interrater reliability coefficients ($r = .86$), which suggests that those differences are based on reliable measurements. Three of the features—body, grammar/mechanics, and style—for which the experimental and control groups did not differ have low interrater reliability, which suggests that the raters may have had trouble scoring these features. For further discussion of the reliability and validity of the results from our classroom experiment, see Liggett, "Preparing Business Writing Students," pp. 58–80.

Notes to Pages 76–80   131

55. Paul B. Diederich, *Measuring Growth in English* (Urbana, IL: NCTE, 1974), p. 33.
56. The memos dictated by the two groups did not appear to differ significantly in the following features: a summary of recommendations early in the memo; a well-organized and developed body; correct use of grammar and mechanics; and an appropriate style. Two explanations may account for the lack of differences between the two groups on these features. Either training in the composing process of dictation was not more effective in preparing students in the treatment group to plan these features, or the measurements used to judge differences were not precise enough. Both explanations are plausible. For example, both groups tended to summarize recommendations early in the memo, which suggests that they relied on previously learned organizing strategies when dictating their memos. Furthermore, both raters strongly agreed when scoring the summary feature. Since this was not the case when they scored the body, grammar and mechanics, and style, it is possible that the measurements may not have been precise enough to detect differences in performance between the two groups on these features. Follow-up studies are needed to investigate further how training in speaking/writing relationships affects a dictator's ability to produce first-time-final memos that are well-organized, grammatically correct, and stylistically appropriate, and to determine more reliable methods for evaluating these features. For further interpretation of these conclusions, see Liggett, "Preparing Business Writing Students," pp. 77–80, 90–92.
57. Northrop Frye, "Communications," in *The Little, Brown Reader*, ed. Marcia Stubbs and Barnet Sylvan (Boston: Little, Brown, 1980), pp. 420–25.

4. The New Technologies Offer Challenging Prospects for Research

1. IABC Teleconference.
2. Panelists for the IABC Teleconference who addressed our question were: Douglas P. Brush, Organizational Communication Consultant, D/J Brush Associates, Cold Springs, NY; Willard Thomas, Chief Executive Officer, Organizational Media Systems, Fort Worth, TX; and Roger D'Aprix, President, Organizational Communication Services, Rochester, NY.
3. Good verbal skills are essential for users of the new communication technology—whether they be high school or college graduates. A su-

pervisor of a New York insurance company estimates that "70% of the insurance firm's correspondence must be corrected and retyped at least once because typists working from dictation don't know how to punctuate sentences and often misspell words." As new technology eliminates rote-typing jobs, secretaries will need better verbal skills (Carol Hymowitz, "Remedial Bosses: Employers Take Over Where Schools Failed to Teach the Basics," *Wall Street Journal*, 22 Jan. 1981, p. 1).

4. Walter J. Ong, "Oral Residue in Tudor Prose Style," in *Rhetoric, Romance, and Technology* (Ithaca, NY: Cornell Univ. Pr., 1971), pp. 23–47.
5. For a general discussion of the impact of the telephone on communication, see I. de Sola Pool, ed., *The Social Impact of the Telephone* (Cambidge, MA: MIT Pr., 1977). For an annotated bibliography of resources for using television in the classroom, see: Shaun S. Smith, "Television and the English Teacher," *English Journal* 68 (Jan. 1979): 76–79. Barbara S. Morris, "The Language Environment of Student Writers," *fforum* 4 (Fall 1982): 84–88, proposes that the incoherent writing style of some students may have been influenced by the disconnected langauge they hear on television, and suggests ways to help student writers transcend the language limitations of television. Her bibliography may prove useful for those interested in conducting research on the effects of television on writing.
6. Faigley and Miller, p. 569.
7. Knoblauch, pp. 155–57; Alan Siegel, "The State of the Language: An Up-to-Date Report on the Plain English Movement" (Paper presented at ABCA International Conference, New Orleans, 21 Oct. 1982).
8. Panelists William O. Coggins, Jane E. Peterson, and Victoria M. Winkler described the value of faculty internships in "Academic, Governmental, and Industrial Interfaces: Channels for Symbiotic Relationships," Conference on College Composition and Communication, Detroit, Mar. 1983. Especially relevant to using faculty internships as a basis for research, curriculum design, and teaching was Winkler's talk, "Telecommunication Systems: Designing and Evaluating Courseware."
9. Raymond Beswick and Peter Clarke, "Business Communication in the Automated Office," preconvention workshop, ABCA International Conference, New Orleans, 20 Oct. 1982.
10. For example, R. C. Crick, "A Technical Communication Procedure to Produce Attitude Change through the Use of Scientifically Designed Messages" (Ph.D. diss., Rensselaer Polytechnic Institute, 1982).
11. Dell Hymes, "Speech and Language: On the Origins and Foundations of Inequality Among Speakers," *Daedalus* 102 (Summer 1973): 68, 70.
12. Loren Barritt, "Writing/Speaking: A Phenomenological View," in *Ex-

ploring Speaking-Writing Relationships: Connections and Contrasts, ed. Barry M. Kroll and Roberta J. Vann (Urbana, IL: NCTE, 1981), pp. 124–33; Gardner, pp. 14, 15, 19; Zinsser, pp. 96–104.
13. See for example: Marilyn Mantei, "Office Automation: After the Installation" (Unpublished paper, Univ. of Michigan, 1982); Alan T. McKenzie, "QWERTYUIOP: Word Processors and the Typing Chores of an English Department," *ADE Bulletin* 63 (Feb. 1980): 18–21; Gardner, pp. 14–15, 19.
14. McWilliams, pp. 92–93.
15. For example, Marie Flatley at San Diego State has developed a business writing course based on sending and receiving assignments through an electronic mail/word processing system, and Donald Payne at Iowa State University uses a word processor with an opaque projector in his writing classes to teach, among other things, revision.
16. Mimi Schwartz, "Computers and the Teaching of Writing," *Educational Technology* 22 (Nov. 1982): 27–29.
17. "Getting Down to the Basics on What Ails the U.S. Economy," interview with Barry P. Bosworth and Martin S. Feldstein, *New York Times*, 8 Nov. 1981, p. 4E; "Office Automation: The Major Issues in Perspective," AFIPS Office Automation Conference, San Francisco, CA, 5 Apr. 1982; Robert A. Shiff, *Impact: Information Technology* 5 (June 1982): 5.
18. "Overcoming Technophobia: Training, Technology and the Communicator," Society for Technical Communication 1983 Spring Symposium, Chicago, 23 Apr. 1983. Speakers from business and industry vividly described the socioeducational implications of introducing the new technologies in the workplace, a subject of current nationwide concern. English teachers would certainly benefit from attending meetings or conferences which address this topic.
19. Personal communications with Andrew Halpern, Stanford Law School, 15 Dec. 1982, and Michael Halpern, Univ. of Michigan, 14 Jan. 1983.
20. Lynn Quitman Troyka describes the nontraditional students we are likely to have in classes in the next few years: "Perspectives on Legacies and Literacy in the 1980s," *College Composition and Communication* 33 (Oct. 1982): 252–62. Also see: James Michels, "Teaching Reading and Writing to Adults with Audio Cassette Tapes," *College Composition and Communication* 33 (Oct. 1982): 317–20; James R. East and Ronald Strahl, "Learn and Shop: Teaching Composition in Shopping Centers," *College Composition and Communication* 33 (Oct. 1982): 267–75; and Dwight Stevenson, "Consulting in Technical Writing in Japan" (Paper presented at Conference on College Composition and Communication, Detroit, Mar. 1983).

21. You can make a Möbius strip by taking a rectangular strip of paper, twisting one end 180 degrees, and taping it to the other end. It looks like this:

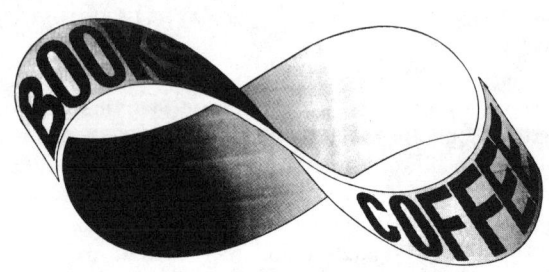

22. Ong, *Interfaces*, p. 90.

Appendixes

1. The process of dictation documented in appendix C is based on our interview data, a close analysis of the notes, tapes, drafts, and final documents of our interviewees, and, to a lesser extent, on our research in secondary sources, especially reports by experienced dictators. To identify the types of communications produced by dictation, we relied on interviewees' comments and the products we collected. To identify the stages and activities of dictated composing, we relied on a combination of research on the composing process (for example, that of Gould, and Flower and Hayes) and on our interviews and collected materials. To estimate the weight given to each activity in each kind of communication, we relied on our interview notes, follow-up discussions with interviewees, and their tapes, drafts, and final products.
2. This segment of the transcribed, edited first draft has been photographically reduced from an 11-by-14 inch printout sheet. It is marked for tape stops, pauses, and other dictation features shown in the annotation key.
3. This sample of a first-time-final letter is reduced from standard 8½-by-11 inch letter size and is marked for tape stops, pauses, and other dictation

features shown in the annotation key. It contains at the top a note to the transcriptionist to add a name to the copy list before mailing.
4. According to the authors' note: "The arrows indicate that *information flows* from one box or process to another; that is, knowledge about the writing assignment or knowledge from memory can be transferred or used in the planning process, and information from planning can flow back the other way. . . . One of the central premises of the cognitive process theory presented here is that writers are constantly, instant by instant, orchestrating a battery of cognitive processes as they integrate planning, remembering, writing, and rereading" (pp. 386–87).
5. Mertes, "Doing Your Office Over," pp. 127–35.
6. Sources for teaching dictation are adapted from Flatley and Vik, p. 139.

Selected Bibliography

Anderson, Richard C. "Schema-directed Processes in Language Comprehension." In *The Psychology of Written Communication*, edited by James Hartley, pp. 33–37. London: Kogan Page, 1980.

Applebee, Arthur N. *Tradition and Reform in the Teaching of English: A History*. Urbana, IL: National Council of Teachers of English, 1974.

Arnold, Carroll C. "Oral Rhetoric, Rhetoric, and Literature." In *Contemporary Rhetoric*, edited by Douglas Ehninger, pp. 65–70. Glenview, IL: Scott, Foresman, 1972.

Barritt, Loren. "Writing/Speaking: A Phenomenological View." In *Exploring Speaking-Writing Relationships: Connections and Contrasts*, edited by Barry M. Kroll and Roberta J. Vann, pp. 124–33. Urbana, IL: NCTE, 1981.

Beaven, Mary H. "Individualized Goal Setting, Self-Evaluation, and Peer Evaluation." In *Evaluating Writing: Describing, Measuring, Judging*, edited by Charles R. Cooper and Lee Odell, pp. 135–56. Urbana, IL: NCTE, 1977.

Brillhart, L. V., and A. Barnett. "Humanizing the Introduction to Computers." In *AEDS Proceedings of 18th Annual Convention: A Gateway to the Use of Computers in Education*, pp. 47–51. Washington, DC: AEDS, 1980.

Britton, James. "The Composing Processes and the Functions of Writing." In *Research on Composing: Points of Departure*, edited by Charles R. Cooper and Lee Odell, pp. 13–28. Urbana, IL: NCTE, 1978.

Britton, James, Tony Burgess, Nancy Martin, Alex McLeod, and Harold Rosen. *The Development of Writing Abilities (11–18)*. London: Macmillian Education Ltd., 1975.

Bruner, Jerome, Jacqueline J. Goodnow, and George A. Austin. *A Study of Thinking*. New York: Wiley, 1956.

Burns, Hugh, and George Culp. "Stimulating Invention in English Composition Through Computer-Assisted Instruction." *Educational Technology* 20 (Aug. 1980): 5–10.

Callaway, Janet. "Coordinating Course Objectives with Assignments, Classroom Methods, and Evaluation Procedures." In *Teaching Business Writing: Approaches, Plans, Pedagogy, Research*, edited by Jeanne W. Halpern, pp. 99–114. Urbana, IL: ABCA, 1983.

Cambourne, Brian. "Oral and Written Relationships: A Reading Perspective." In *Exploring Speaking-Writing Relationships: Connections and Contrasts*, edited by Barry M. Kroll and Roberta J. Vann, pp. 82–98. Urbana, IL:

Collins, James L. "Speaking, Writing, and Teaching for Meaning." In *Exploring Speaking-Writing Relationships: Connections and Contrasts*, edited by Barry M. Kroll and Roberta J. Vann, pp. 198–214. Urbana, IL: NCTE, 1981.

Cooper, Charles R., and Lee Odell, eds. *Evaluating Writing: Describing, Measuring, Judging*. Urbana, IL: NCTE, 1977.

———. *Research on Composing: Points of Departure*. Urbana, IL: NCTE, 1978.

Corbett, Edward P. J. *Classical Rhetoric for the Modern Student*. 2d ed. New York: Oxford Univ. Pr., 1971.

———. "What Is Being Revived?" *College Composition and Communication* 18 (Oct. 1967): 166–72.

"Dictation Today: Voices of the Users." *Modern Office Procedures* (March 1979), p. 70.

Diederich, Paul B. *Measuring Growth in English*. Urbana, IL: NCTE, 1974.

Dixon, John. *Growth Through English*. London: Oxford Univ. Pr., 1967.

Elbow, Peter. *Writing Without Teachers*. New York: Oxford Univ. Pr., 1973.

Ellis, Clarence A., and Gary J. Nutt. "Office Information Systems and Computer Science." *Computer Surveys* 12 (Mar. 1980): 27–60.

Emig, Janet. "Writing as a Mode of Learning." *College Composition and Communication* 28 (May 1977): 122–28.

Faigley, Lester, and Thomas P. Miller. "What We Learn from Writing on the Job." *College English* 44 (Oct. 1982): 557–69.

Farrell, Edmund J. *English, Education, and the Electronic Revolution*. Urbana, IL: NCTE, 1967.

Ferrill, June O. "Devising New Courses for New Clientele." In *Teaching Business Writing: Approaches, Plans, Pedagogy, Research*, edited by Jeanne W. Halpern, pp. 52–65. Urbana, IL: ABCA, 1983.

Fitts, Paul, and Michael Posner. *Human Performance*. Belmont, CA: Brooks/Cole, 1968.

Flatley, Marie E., and Gretchen Vik. "Incorporating Oral Communication and Dictation Skills in Business Writing Classes." In *Teaching Business Writing: Approaches, Plans, Pedagogy, Research*, edited by Jeanne W. Halpern, pp. 129–45. Urbana, IL: ABCA, 1983.

Flower, Linda. *Problem-Solving Strategies for Writing*. New York: Harcourt, 1981.

———. "Writer-Based Prose: A Cognitive Basis for Problems in Writing." *College English* 41 (Sept. 1979): 19–38.

Flower, Linda, and John R. Hayes. "A Cognitive Process Theory of Writing." *College Composition and Communication* 32 (Dec. 1981): 365–87.

———. "The Dynamics of Composing: Making Plans and Juggling Constraints." In *Cognitive Processes in Writing*, edited by Lee W. Gregg and Erwin R. Steinberg, pp. 31–50. Hillsdale, NJ: Lawrence Erlbaum, 1980.

Foster, Harold M. *The New Literacy: The Language of Film and Television*. Urbana, IL: NCTE, 1979.

Gardner, Howard. "On Becoming a Dictator." *Psychology Today* 14 (Dec. 1980): 14–15, 19.

Gere, Anne Ruggles. "A Cultural Perspective on Talking and Writing." In *Exploring Speaking-Writing Relationships: Connections and Contrasts*, edited by Barry M. Kroll and Roberta J. Vann, pp. 111–23. Urbana, IL: NCTE, 1981.

Gibson, James W., Charles R. Gruner, Robert J. Kibler, and Francis J. Kelly. "A Quantitative Examination of Differences and Similarities in Written and Spoken Messages." *Speech Monographs* 33 (Nov. 1966): 444–51.

Gould, John D. "Experiments on Composing Letters: Some Facts, Some Myths, and Some Observations." In *Cognitive Processes in Writing*, edited by Lee W. Gregg and Erwin R. Steinberg, pp. 97–127. Hillsdale, NJ: Lawrence Erlbaum, 1980.

Gregg, Lee W., and Erwin R. Steinberg, eds. *Cognitive Processes in Writing*. Hillsdale, NJ: Lawrence Erlbaum, 1980.

Halpern, Jeanne W. "What Should We Be Teaching Students in Business Writing?" *Journal of Business Communication* 18 (Summer 1981): 37–53.

———. ed. *Teaching Business Writing: Approaches, Plans, Pedagogy, Research*. Urbana, IL: ABCA, 1983.

Halpern, Jeanne W., and Dale Matthews. "Helping Inexperienced Writers: An Informal Discussion with Mina Shaughnessy." *English Journal* 69 (Mar. 1980): 32–37.

Hartley, James, ed. *The Psychology of Written Communication*. London: Kogan Page, 1980.

Hirsch, E. D., Jr. *The Philosophy of Composition*. Chicago: Univ. of Chicago Pr., 1977.

Hymowitz, Carol. "Remedial Bosses: Employers Take Over Where Schools Failed to Teach the Basics." *Wall Street Journal*, 22 Jan. 1981, p. 1.

Joos, Martin. *The Five Clocks*. New York: Harcourt, 1961.

Knoblauch, C. H. "Intentionality in the Writing Process: A Case Study." *College Composition and Communication* 31 (May 1980): 153–59.

Koch, Carl, and James M. Brazil. *Strategies for Teaching the Composition Process*. Urbana, IL: NCTE, 1978.

Kroll, Barry M. "Developmental Relationships between Speaking and Writing." In *Exploring Speaking-Writing Relationships: Connections and Contrasts*, edited by Barry M. Kroll and Roberta J. Vann, pp. 32–54. Urbana, IL: NCTE, 1981.

Kroll, Barry M., and Roberta J. Vann, eds. *Exploring Speaking-Writing Relationships: Connections and Contrasts*. Urbana, IL: NCTE, 1981.

Larson, Richard L. "Structure and Form in Non-Fiction Prose." In *Teaching Composition: 10 Bibliographical Essays*, edited by Gary Tate, pp. 45–71. Fort Worth, TX: Texas Christian Univ. Pr., 1976.

Lauer, Janice. "Toward a Metatheory of Heuristic Procedures." *College Composition and Communication* 30 (Oct. 1979): 248–69.

Lauer, Janice, Gene Montague, Andrea Lunsford, and Janet Emig. *Four Worlds of Writing*. New York: Harper, 1981.

Lee, Patrick. "Bouncing Around a Good Idea: Satellite Videoconferencing." *California Business* (Feb. 1982), pp. 40–41, 60, 79.

Liggett, Sarah. "Preparing Business Writing Students to Use Dictation Systems: An Experimental Study." Ph.D. diss., Purdue Univ., 1982.

―――. "Relationships Between Speaking and Writing: An Annotated Bibliography" *College Composition and Communication*, forthcoming.

Lunsteen, Sara. *Listening*. Urbana, IL: NCTE, 1979.

Luria, Aleksandr R., and F. I. Yudovich. *Speech and the Development of Mental Processes in the Child*. Edited by Joan Simon. Baltimore: Penguin, 1971.

Mathes, J. C., and Dwight Stevenson. *Designing Technical Reports: Writing for Audiences in Organizations*. Indianapolis: Bobbs-Merrill, 1976.

Matsuhashi, Ann. "Pausing and Planning: The Tempo of Written Discourse Production." *Research in the Teaching of English* 15 (May 1981): 113–34.

Mayer, Kenneth R., and Bella G. Clinkscale. "Developing Dictation Competencies in Collegiate Business Communication Courses." In *Unfurling Communication's Colors in the 80's: Proceedings, 1980 ABCA National Conference*, edited by Sam J. Bruno, pp. 23–36. Urbana, IL: ABCA, 1980.

McKenzie, Alan T. "QWERTYUIOP: Word Processors and the Typing Chores of an English Department." *ADE Bulletin* 63 (Feb. 1980): 18–21.

McLuhan, Marshall. *Understanding Media: The Extensions of Man*. New York: McGraw, 1965.

McLuhan, Marshall, and Quentin Fiore. *The Medium is the Massage*. New York: Bantam, 1967.

McWilliams, Peter A. *The Word Processing Book: A Short Course in Computer Literacy*. Los Angeles: Prelude Pr., 1982.

Mertes, Louis H. "Doing Your Office Over—Electronically." *Harvard Business Review* 59 (Mar.–Apr. 1981): 127–35.

———. "The Professional Environment in the 21st Century." *Computerworld* 15 (1 Sept. 1981): 31–38.

Meyer, Bonnie J. F. "Reading Research and the Composition Teacher: The Importance of Plans." *College Composition and Communication* 33 (Feb. 1982): 37–49.

Moffett, James. *Active Voice*. Montclair, NJ: Boynton/Cook, 1981.

———. *Teaching the Universe of Discourse*. Boston: Houghton, 1968.

Murray, Donald M. "Internal Revision: A Process of Discovery." In *Research on Composing: Points of Departure*, edited by Charles R. Cooper and Lee Odell, pp. 85–103. Urbana, IL: NCTE, 1978.

Nancarrow, Paula Reed, Donald Ross, and Lillian Bridwell. *Word Processors and the Writing Process: An Annotated Bibliography*. Minneapolis: English Dept., Univ. of Minnesota, 1982.

Odell, Lee. "Redefining 'Mature Writing.'" Unpublished paper. Albany: State Univ. of New York, 1979.

———. "Teachers of Composition and Needed Research in Discourse Theory." *College Composition and Communication* 30 (Feb. 1979): 39–45.

Odell, Lee, and Dixie Goswami. "Writing in a Non-Academic Setting." *Research in the Teaching of English* 16 (Oct. 1982): 201–23.

Olson, David R. "Writing: The Divorce of the Author from the Text." In *Exploring Speaking-Writing Relationships: Connections and Contrasts*, edited by Barry M. Kroll and Roberta J. Vann, pp. 99–110. Urbana, IL: NCTE, 1981.

Ong, Walter J. *Interfaces of the Word: Studies in the Evolution of Consciousness and Culture*. Ithaca, NY: Cornell Univ. Pr., 1977.

―――. "Literacy and Orality in Our Times." In *Profession 79*, pp. 1–7. New York: Modern Language Association, 1979.

―――. *Orality and Literacy: The Technologizing of the Word*. New York: Methuen, 1982.

―――. *Rhetoric, Romance, and Technology*. Ithaca, NY: Cornell Univ. Pr., 1971.

Payne, Don. "Integrating Oral and Written Business Communication." In *Exploring Speaking-Writing Relationships: Connections and Contrasts*, edited by Barry M. Knoll and Roberta J. Vann, pp. 184–97. Urbana, IL: NCTE, 1981.

Pearsall, Thomas. *Audience Analysis for Technical Writers*. Beverly Hills, CA: Glenco Pr., 1969.

Perham, John. "Business' New Communication Tool." *Dun's Review* 117 (Feb. 1981): 80–82.

Perl, Sondra. "Understanding Composing." *College Composition and Communication* 31 (Dec. 1980): 363–69.

Postman, Neil. *Television and the Teaching of English*. New York: Appleton, 1961.

Radar, Martha H., and Alan P. Wunsch. "A Survey of Communication Practices of Business School Graduates by Job Category and Undergraduate Major." *Journal of Business Communication* 17 (Summer 1980): 33–41.

Radcliffe, Terry. "Talk-Write Composition: A Theoretical Model Proposing the Use of Speech to Improve Writing." *Research in the Teaching of English* 6 (Fall 1972): 189–99.

Ricks, Betty R. "The Neglected Managerial Communication Skills." *ABCA Bulletin* 44 (Dec. 1981): 22–25.

Rogers, Don. *Executive Dictation Cookbook*. Atlanta: Lanier, 1979.

Schafer, John C. "The Linguistic Analysis of Spoken and Written Texts." In *Exploring Speaking-Writing Relationships: Connections and Contrasts*, edited by Barry M. Kroll and Roberta J. Vann, pp. 1–31. Urbana, IL: NCTE, 1981.

Schwartz, Mimi. "Computers and the Teaching of Writing." *Educational Technology* 22 (Nov. 1982): 27–29.

Selzer, Jack. "Readability Is a Four-Letter Word." *Journal of Business Communication* 18 (Fall 1981): 21–32.

Sommers, Nancy. "Revision Strategies of Student Writers and Experienced Adult Writers." *College Composition and Communication* 31 (Dec. 1980): 378–88.

Spiro, Rand J. "Remembering Information from Text: Theoretical and Empirical Issues Concerning the 'State of Schema' Reconstruction Hypothesis." In *Schooling and the Acquisition of Knowledge*, edited by Richard C. Anderson, Rand J. Spiro, and William E. Montague, pp. 137–65. Hillsdale, NJ: Lawrence Erlbaum, 1977.

Stallard, Charles K. "An Analysis of the Writing of Good Student Writers." *Research in the Teaching of English* 8 (Summer 1974): 206–18.

Stein, Judith, and JoAnne Yates. "Electronic Mail: How Will It Change Office Communication? Can Managers Use It Effectively?" In *Information Systems and Business Communication*, edited by Alfred B. Williams. Urbana, IL: ABCA, forthcoming.

Tate, Gary, ed. *Teaching Composition: 10 Bibliographical Essays*. Fort Worth, TX: Texas Christian Univ. Pr., 1976.

Toffler, Alvin. *The Third Wave*. New York: Bantam, 1980.

Tovatt, Anthony, and Elbert L. Miller. "Oral-Aural-Visual Stimuli Approach to Teaching Written Composition to 9th Grade Students." ERIC, Document ED 015 204, 1967.

———. "The Sound of Writing." *Research in the Teaching of English* 1 (Fall 1967): 176–89.

Troyka, Lynn Quitman. "Perspectives on Legacies and Literacy in the 1980s." *College Composition and Communication* 33 (Oct. 1982): 252–62.

Van Dyke, Barrie. "On-the-Job Writing of High Level Business Executives." Paper presented at Conference on College Composition and Communication, Washington, Mar. 1980.

Vygotsky, Lev S. *Thought and Language*. Edited and translated by Eugenia Hanfmann and Gertrude Vakar. Cambridge, MA: MIT Pr., 1962.

Wall, Shavaun M., and Nancy E. Taylor. "Using Interactive Computer Programs in Teaching Higher Conceptual Skills: An Approach to Instruction in Writing." *Educational Technology* 22 (Feb. 1982): 13–17.

Williams, Alfred B., ed. *Information Systems and Business Communication*. Urbana, IL: ABCA, forthcoming.

Williams, Frederick. *The Communications Revolution*. Beverly Hills, CA: Sage, 1982.

Williams, Joseph M. *Style: Ten Lessons in Clarity and Grace*. Glenview, IL: Scott, Foresman, 1981.

Winkler, Victoria M. "Telecommunication Systems: Designing and Evaluating Courseware." Paper presented at Conference on College Composition and Communication, Detroit, Mar. 1983.

Winterowd, W. Ross. "Transferable and Local Writing Skills." *Journal of Advanced Composition* 1 (Spring 1980): 1–3.

Witte, Stephen P., and Lester Faigley. "Coherence, Cohesion, and Writing Quality." *College Composition and Communication* 32 (May 1981): 189–204.

Wresch, William. "Computers in English Class: Finally Beyond Grammar and Spelling Drills." *College English* 44 (Sept. 1982): 483–90.

Young, Richard E. "Designing Objectives for Teaching Technical Writing Courses." In *Proceedings: Program in Technical and Professional Communication*, pp. 95–98. Ann Arbor, MI, Aug. 1981.

———. "Paradigms and Problems: Needed Research in Rhetorical Invention." In *Research on Composing: Points of Departure*, edited by Charles R. Cooper and Lee Odell, pp. 29–47. Urbana, IL: NCTE, 1978.

Zinsser, William. *Writing with a Word Processor*. New York: Harper, 1983.

Zoellner, Robert. "Talk-Write: A Behavioral Pedagogy for Composition." *College English* 30 (Jan. 1969): 267–320.

Zoerner, C. E., Jr. "A Survey of Great Dictators." *ABCA Bulletin* 44 (Mar. 1981): 7–9.